# The Advanced Day Trading Guide

**Learn Secret Step by Step Strategies on How You Can Day Trade Forex, Options, Stocks, and Futures to Become a Successful Day Trader for a Living!**

By Neil Sharp

# Table of Contents

**Table of Contents**
**Introduction**
**Chapter 1: The fundamentals of day trading**

Characteristics of a day trader

Characteristic #1: Discipline
Characteristic #2: Patience
Characteristic #3: Flexibility
Characteristic #4: Resiliency
Characteristic #5: Independence
Characteristic #6: Vision

Day trading as a full-time career

The day trading differs from other types of trading
Benefits of day trading
Drawbacks of day trading
Basics of day trading futures
Day trading FOREX
Day trading options
Day trading equities

**Chapter 2: Trading basics**

Bid and Ask
Types of Orders

**Chapter 3: Setting up a brokerage account**

Overview
Fees
Account Minimums
Requirements
Cash or margin

How to open an account
Advantages of brokerage accounts
What to watch out for

## Chapter 4: How to choose the right stocks

Company revenue
Earnings per share
Return on Equity
Assets (-) liabilities = equity
Analyst recommendations
Positive earnings
Earnings forecast
Earnings growth
PEG Ratio
Industry price earnings
Days to cover

## Chapter 5: The best time to trade

Overview
Market opening
Market closing
Avoiding pitfalls

## Chapter 6: Reducing risk in day trading

Determining the right amount of investable capital
Setting up a stop-loss point
Working with a broker
Taking breaks when needed
Keeping emotions in check
Avoiding fads

## Chapter 7: Day trading strategies

Candlestick charting

Bullish candlesticks
Bearish candlesticks
The ABCD pattern
Reverse trading
Moving average trend trading
Resistance trading
Opening range breakout
Red to green trading
Data analysis in trading
Technical analysis in day trading
The bottom line

## Chapter 8: Advanced trading strategies

Gap up, inside Bar, breakout strategy
Gap up, attempt to fill, breakout
The gap up, afternoon breakout
Fibonacci retracement pattern
Gap down, fill down, inside bar, breakout

## Chapter 9: Tips for completing a successful trade

Building up a watch list
Deciding on the right stocks for you
Putting an entry and exit strategy into place
Purchasing desired stocks
Paying attention to the market until the trade is completed
Selling stocks when reaching original exit points
Reflecting on trades and extracting lessons learned
Researching information for future trades
Automating trade processes

## Conclusion

# Introduction

Thank you for buying "*The Advanced Day Trading Guide: Learn Secret Step by Step Strategies on How You Can Day Trade Forex, Options, Stocks, and Futures to Become a Successful Day Trader for a Living!*" I greatly appreciate the interest you have taken in learning more on how you can become a successful day trader.

This book is a guide which will help you to make up your mind, once and for all, on becoming a day trader for a living.

I know that you have a lot of questions. And, I also know that you may be unsure if this is the right job for you.

The fact is that day trading has enabled many individuals to become financially independent and provide for their families while getting away from the rat race.

I know that might sound too good to be true.

But it's not.

It's a dream that many of us have had. But only a few of us have been able to make it come true. Now, it's your turn to make it real.

How can you become a successful day trader for a living?

Well, that's what this guide is about!

In this guide, you will learn about every aspect that you need to know in order to make your first trade.

Also, I have taken great care in ensuring that the information contained herein is relevant and up to date. So, you can rest assured that you will be getting solid advice on investing in financial markets.

I would also encourage you to follow up on the information in this book.

Since constant research and learning are two fundamental actions of successful traders, I would encourage you to find as many sources of information as you can in order to make informed decisions.

With that in mind, let's find out what information is available to you so that you may build a killer investment strategy.

I hope you are as eager as I am to get started.

So, here we go!

## Chapter 1: The fundamentals of day trading

Day trading is just like any other career you could choose. However, not many folks understand how it works. You may have heard many people talk about how potentially lucrative it can be. In fact, you may even know someone who has made a living out of day trading.

In this chapter, we're going to be taking a closer look at how you can make day trading a full-time career which can not only pay for your basic needs and help fund your lifestyle. In addition, day trading can become lucrative enough to fund your retirement. More importantly, day trading is a means for you to achieve financial freedom and security.

So, let's take a closer look at what it takes to become a successful day trader.

## Characteristics of a day trader

In order to become a successful day trader, an individual needs to have six basic traits. These traits will enable a day trader to become successful and the chief the results they are looking to produce.

**Characteristic #1: Discipline**

Discipline is by far the most important trait that any day trader can have. Discipline is what enables a day-trader to maintain focus during their day-to-day activities. In addition, focus is very important when market conditions are adverse.

By being disciplined, a day trader can be sure that they will be consistent in the way they carry out their investment strategy. This is very important since developing a solid investment strategy is not enough to become successful if the traitor cannot be consistent and stick to it.

Also, discipline is about establishing a routine and being able to follow through on the objectives set forth at the outset. Successful day traders are able to set up schedule and consistently carry out the activities that will lead them to identifying potential opportunities such as conducting research on a regular basis.

However, discipline isn't just about establishing a routine and following through on an investment plan. Discipline is also about having the restraint to avoid following trends and falling into psychological pitfalls. For example, a hot stock might be sought after by many investors. Therefore, discipline can be exercised in refraining from jumping in headfirst along with other investors who are driving up the price indiscriminately.

Discipline is also manifest in an investor's attitude by understanding that investment opportunities require a specific amount of research and time to develop. This approach implies resisting the temptation of hitting a home run or finding a magic bullet. Of course, there is always the temptation of trying to make one huge train that can make you rich. While that is certainly possible, it is highly unlikely.

Consequently, day traders must have the discipline to do nothing when there are no good opportunities available, and they must also have the discipline to act with prudence when allocating their resources into potential Investments.

Another important aspect of discipline is respecting the buy and sell points set forth in an investment strategy. When evaluating a potential investment, investors must be disciplined enough to purchase when the price falls to their expected level and not before. In addition, investors must exercise even more discipline in selling when an investment reaches their target sell point. As such, discipline is perhaps the most important factor when making a decision to sell.

When selling, there is always the expectation that the price of an investment may go up further. So, discipline enables an investor to sell at a point where they will feel comfortable with their returns and avoid waiting too long and possibly missing out on a great opportunity.

The same can be said about purchasing. Discipline is a great way of counteracting a phenomenon known as "the fear of missing out." The fear of missing out consists in wanting to take advantage of investment opportunities that will yield considerable results. Thus, an individual may jump into an investment simply because they must act quickly lest they miss a great investment opportunity. This rash behavior can lead to risky Investments and exposure to potential losses.

**Characteristic #2: Patience**

The second characteristic that we will discuss is patience.

Patience is the perfect partner to discipline. What discipline, patience is about an Investor's attitude. Most individuals are looking to get rich quick. This is especially true when individual investors have ambitious goals and targets they wish to meet as soon as possible. And while there's nothing wrong with wanting to get ahead quickly, a lack of patience may cloud and investors judgment.

Patience is a virtue.

Patience is what distinguishes mature and savvy traders from reckless and immature ones. A lack of patience can lead investors to making poor choices regarding investment opportunities. This is true in cases where markets, or any other type of investments, are "hot." In such cases, other investors may be manipulating the price of a stock, asset, or commodity, to a point where other investors believe the time to act is now.

It is certainly possible to find yourself in a position where you must act quickly. Nevertheless, patience is a key factor in understanding that it might not be the best moment to get into that particular investment. In fact, you may have to exercise patience in order to wait for a stock to fall to the price that you have sent in your investment strategy. Likewise, you must exercise patience in waiting for a stock's value to rise to a point where you feel comfortable in selling.

A word of caution on being patient: investors often confuse being patient with holding on to an investment for too long. In this case, you might find yourself in a position where you may have to cut your losses. When you find yourself in a position where an investment does not seem likely to rebound after a string of losses, it might be best the dump that stock and cut your losses.

However, if you were considering a more long-term approach, then you may have to exercise even more patience in waiting for your investments to rebound. A good example of this is when you have invested in a mutual fund or an index fund. These funds are typically tied to a market's overall performance. Therefore, you may need to wait for the market to ride out a downturn so that you can begin to make money again.

At the end of the day, it all boils down to having a clear investment strategy which can outline the parameters by which you will hold your decisions accountable to. Patience is the trait that will enable you to keep a cool head while markets and individual assets go through the typical ups and downs that come with trading financial assets.

**Characteristic #3: Flexibility**

Another key characteristic that we will discuss in this chapter is flexibility.

Flexibility is one of the most important characteristics an investor can possess. Flexibility is about the attitude which, in essence, means rolling with the punches. Unlike other careers, investing in financial markets and instruments is a highly unpredictable and volatile endeavor. This is especially true when markets are under uncertain economic conditions. These uncertain conditions can become further compounded by an unclear political landscape.

This is why investors must always have an open mind. By being flexible and adaptable, investors can see the forest for the trees. They will be able to analyze and understand the data in front of them and realize where market trends are heading. In that regard, understanding data in market trends will enable investors to adjust their strategies accordingly.

Let's consider an example.

An investor has set a short-term strategy in which this investor has decided to get into an oil ETF. Current market analysis supposes that oil prices will remain stable for the foreseeable future. At the very least, fluctuations in oil prices are not expected to be significant for the remainder of the year. Suddenly, political instability has hit one of the major oil-producing countries. This implies a significant shift in the outlook for oil prices. The new outlook for oil prices contemplates a significant jump in prices.

This scenario presents potential investment decisions.

The first would be to buy further into the current oil ETF. Since the outlook is for prices to increase significantly, allocating further resources into the oil ETF would lead to further gains. This seems like a logical and reasonable investment decision.

The second investment decision would be to hold the current investment position in the oil ETF and wait for the market to skyrocket. At that point, an investor would consider selling their position in that ETF and collecting their winnings.

Both of the investment decisions presented here would pocket an investor a considerable sum of money. While the original strategy might have called for holding the opposition until the end of the year, the sudden change in oil production has caused a significant shift in oil prices. So, a savvy investor will be able to recognize the need to shift strategies and take advantage of the new developments.

Conversely, consider the decision of major oil-producing countries to increase their oil output and thereby bring oil prices down. Again, the original investment decision was to hold the position until the end of the year. Due to these new developments, an investor may choose to get rid of their position in the oil ETF at once.

The lesson in the previous example is that investors must keep their eyes and ears open at all times. Consequently, investors must be ready to act when needed and keep an open mind with regard to adjusting their investment strategies. It's important to note that investment strategies should never be cast in stone. As a matter of fact, investment strategies should be taken for what they are: a road map which shows different ways to get to the same destination.

**Characteristic #4: Resiliency**

The next characteristic that we will discuss is resiliency.

Resiliency is a fundamental trait in any trader. Resiliency is key because it is part of an investor's mindset in which obstacles and setbacks will not stop them from staying on course. Resiliency is as much about being mentally tough as it is putting failures and setbacks in the past.

Trading is just like life. Life is filled with many ups and downs. The problem is not failing or losing. The problem is how you can bounce back from a negative experience. Resilient individuals will take failures and losses as learning experiences. They will derive important understanding that will enable them to be successful in the future.

In contrast, those individuals who are not resilient will allow a setback to bring them down. These individuals are the kind that starts something and leaves it as soon as it gets tough — as such, being resilient is about staying the course even when things get very tough.

However, being resilient does not imply that an investor should continue making the same trade or investing in the same vehicles when losses or adverse market conditions are clearly apparent. In fact, a losing trade may be a signal that it is time to shift focus into another stock or another type of investment. This is where a negative experience will enable them to learn an important lesson.

Furthermore, slumps and losing streaks are also common in trading. A good example are professional athletes. Even high-performance athletes will run into the occasional slump and losing streak. When this occurs, top-level athletes will go back to the drawing board and try to understand what's not working right in order to go back to their winning ways.

The same attitude holds true for investors. An investor who suddenly hits the wall and finds himself in the middle of a slump would do well to go back to the drawing board and revisit the original investment strategy. From there, important lessons learned can be derived. These lessons may include an understanding of what has changed or what's not working well. Then, an investor can choose to make the changes that they consider appropriate.

One important consideration of resiliency is that investors need not be perfect. As a matter of fact, an investor can lose half the time and still build significant wealth. The trick to ensuring that an investor will build wealth in spite of losses is to hedge risk as much as possible. That is, if a trade goes bad then the losses from that trade should not cripple an investor's financial position.

In addition, consistency is very important. A trader who consistently gets good results will most assuredly get ahead in the investment game. So, the next time you take a loss, don't get discouraged. Take it for what it is: a learning opportunity and move on.

### Characteristic #5: Independence

The next characteristic we will discuss is independence.

Independence is about not depending on anything, or anyone, to make decisions. Now, this doesn't mean taking on the world alone. What it means is that an investor should be free to act on their own.

Naturally, we all need help when we first set out to do something. A good example of that is this book. You have acknowledged that you don't know everything or may need a nudge in the right direction. So, this book seeks to provide the direction you need in order to become successful at trading.

Furthermore, being successful at training is a lifelong learning process. No one will ever know everything there is to know about trading. That means there was always something new that you can learn. Based on that, you can take classes, courses, seminars, or just read as much as you can on the topic. By being independent, you will be able to process all the information around you and make a logical decision based on the information that's available to you.

When an investor is dependent on professional advice or other means and methods that will essentially make decisions for them, it would be best for this investor to surrender decisions to a money manager. In this case, the money manager will be in charge of allocating investable resources into assets and Investments they consider to be appropriate.

However, the main purpose of becoming a day trader is to gain independence and liberty of action. Unlike traditional stockbrokers, day traders do not work in an office and do not hold themselves accountable to a boss who dictates their actions. It is true that most stockbrokers have some leeway, day traders have all the leeway in the world. This is why the first characteristic in the section, discipline, is the first and foremost characteristic a day trader must possess.

Independence is also about being free to think for yourself. Many investors succumb to the opinions of so-called financial experts on television and the internet. An independent investor will be able to listen to these pundits' opinions and determine whether they are right or whether they are not.

Furthermore, independent investors will not go with the flow. They will not get into "hot" Investments just because everyone is getting into them. An independent investor will be able to determine if popular market trends are Justified or if they are just fads fueled by irrational behavior.

At the end of the day, a successful investor will maintain an independent view about their investment strategy while keeping their emotions in check. This attitude will most assuredly enable investors to keep a cool head at all times.

**Characteristic #6: Vision**

The final characteristic in this section is vision.

Vision is a fundamental trait that all investors must possess. This one is about forward-thinking. That is, having the foresight and recognizing where market trends are leading. Of course, no one has a crystal ball that can predict the future. Savvy investors reach a point where they can make reasonable assumptions based on available data at a given point in time.

Vision is also about seeing future investment opportunities. For example, those investors who saw the internet early on as a potentially worthwhile investment opportunity made a killing when the internet took off. Similarly, visionary investors are able to detect companies that may be underperforming or haven't hit their stride yet. When they do, they're able to get into investments at an early stage. When these investments take off, visionary investors are lauded for being forward-thinking individuals who found value where others were unable to.

This is why I always say that being an investor means keeping your head in the clouds. Now, that doesn't mean that your feet should not be planted firmly on the ground. That's hardly the case. The fact of the matter is that investors must dream. Investors must dream about what the future holds. Based on that assumption, investors can use their better judgment to identify those potential opportunities which could lead to significant gains down the road.

So, the next time you're considering making a trade, think about where that stock or asset is heading.

Is this just a short-term trade that will help you pocket some cash or is this a trade that could lead to bigger and better things in the future? Whatever your answer may be, you will be able to make wise decisions based on your experience and clear judgement.

## Day trading as a full-time career

Day trading is just like any other career. It requires a commitment in both time and effort en route to becoming successful at it.

What differentiates day trading from other careers is that it isn't exactly a job.

Allow me to explain.

A regular job, whatever it may be, positions an individual to trade their time and efforts in exchange for a wage. The employer purchases the talents and time of their employees so they can help achieve the ultimate goal of their enterprise.

On the other hand, day trading, while potentially lucrative, does not offer a steady paycheck. This is not the type of activity that complacent individuals may choose to engage in. If anything, day trading is filled with many ups and downs.

Despite the uncertain nature of trading in financial markets, day trading can become a full-time career. In order for this to happen, an individual investor must become successful at it to a point where they are able to generate enough income to cover basic expenses. Once basic expenses have been covered, ongoing investment activity aims to become a feedback loop in which the proceeds from successful investments feed on themselves and enable an investor's wealth to multiply.

It is very much a possibility to make day trading a full-time career. I do not advocate individual to quit their job today and dive headfirst into investment trading. This is why I recommend a more gradual approach. You can start out by trading in your free time rebuilding momentum. Once you are able to cover your basic expenses on a consistent, month-to-month basis, you might consider making this transition.

**The day trading differs from other types of trading**

Day trading, as its name indicates, consists an opening and closing position within one trading day. Consequently, the investor begins the trading day with a set amount of investable capital, invests the amount that the trader considers pertinent, makes trades, then closes all position prior to the end of the trading day. This means that when the trading day is over, the investor has cashed out. As such, day traders live day by day. In short, day traders carry out the ultimate short-term trading strategy.

Other types of trading include swing trading. Swing trading consists of traders who keep their positions open for longer than one day, but generally less than a few days. On average, swing trades range from 2 to 6 days. Based on that premise, short-term traders play the swings on the market. Swing traders tend to live on the edge in times of high market volatility.

Furthermore, day traders do not engage in long-term investments. This may include purchasing long-term ETFs, mutual funds, certificates of deposit, and so on. These investments would be considered long-term if they exceed one month.

In any event, day traders may purchase other long-term investment products are a means of allocating investable funds for the long run. In particular, these investment vehicles can be used toward funding retirement plans.

**Benefits of day trading**

Day trading offers a series of benefits when taken upon as a full-time job.

Benefits include:

- Flexibility in time and scheduling
- Freedom of action
- Option to work from home
- Option to work from anywhere in the world

- No bosses
- Ability to take time off when needed

Undoubtedly, becoming a day trader may sound too good to be true. After all, the prospect of getting out of the rat race, making a decent living, providing for the family and enjoying freedom of action are all great perks that come with an occupation such as this one.

Successful day traders are able to focus their work for certain periods of time, and then take time off as needed. Since day trading implies closing positions at the end of the day, there is no need to track investments over time. In fact, it is quite reassuring to know that you won't have any surprises when you wake up in the morning.

One other significant advantage of day trading is that you will be able to react quickly when market conditions change. Thus, if markets suddenly swing, you will be able to make adjustments accordingly. Longer-term investors made end up taking longer to react thereby exposing themselves to market volatility.

Consequently, day traders must be on top of everything when they are "on." Once they are "off," they can sit back and reap the rewards of a day's work.

### Drawbacks of day trading

As with anything in life, the bad comes with the good.

Since day trading is not a job in the traditional sense, the freedom that comes with being your own boss comes without a steady paycheck. While more risk-averse folks would cringe at the thought of not having a steady paycheck every month, day traders expose themselves to risking their financial well-being during hard times.

Also, day trading may end up being a high-stress proposition during hard times. This is especially true when markets are trending downward. In addition, day trading may offer limited opportunities during a bear market or in times of recession. Nevertheless, hard times might present a good opportunity for finding hidden value.

Furthermore, day traders must exhibit the personal traits that we discussed earlier in this chapter. When traders lack discipline, patience or vision, they may find it difficult to execute an effective trading strategy. So, if an individual does not exhibit these characteristics, they will have a greater chance of failing.

One other important point to consider is your tax strategy. I would advocate consulting with a tax expert such as an accountant or CPA in order to determine what tax advantages may be utilized in order to protect your earnings. For instance, you might consider incorporation so that your trading activity is done by a legal entity and not you, personally. Incorporation offers a series of tax benefits that individuals do not usually get. This is why it's best to consult with a tax expert.

**Basics of day trading futures**

Futures contracts are a type of derivative in which the underlying asset of the contract is paid for in advance of its delivery. Futures deal almost exclusively in commodities though there may be futures contracts in other assets such as currency. Futures are generally traded on all major stock exchanges around the world. Therefore, futures are not just limited to one specific exchange.

Since futures deal with assets whose price fluctuates according to market conditions, keeping open positions for a longer period of time may expose investors to sudden market fluctuations. For instances, oil futures tend to be the riskiest of all.

Since day trading implies opening and closing positions in the same day, investors can avoid the ups and downs that come with leaving positions overnight. In addition, futures are often traded after the close of markets in the United States. That implies that fluctuations in Asian markets will have a direct impact of futures traded in the United States.

So, if oil futures fall during trading in Asia, an investor in North America may wake up to an unpleasant surprise. By cashing out at the end of the day, day traders can ensure that there will be no surprised at the beginning of the next trading day.

Advanced day traders may choose to keep positions open overnight. However, derivatives are the riskiest type of investment vehicles. This is why it's vital for investors to be absolutely clear on the advantages and disadvantages that come with dabbling in these markets.

**Day trading FOREX**

FOREX deals exclusively in trading currency. In essence, FOREX pits one currency against another. So, the rise or fall in the valuation of a currency would imply a gain or loss in another.

Trading currency is extremely volatile and can lead to considerable fluctuations in a short period of time. In particular, trading currencies of emerging countries can mean serious business. If caught unawares, an investor can be wiped out in the FOREX market.

Day trading eliminates a great deal of exposure since opening, and closing positions on a daily basis would enable investors to manage risk. For instance, if an investor invests in US Dollars and Euros, the time difference between North America and Europe can expose investors to considerable fluctuations overnight.

Trading in FOREX is a potentially lucrative activity during significant market swings. FOREX traders can make considerable profits when one currency is seriously devalued over another. Nevertheless, day traders are better positioned at reaping the benefits of FOREX trading since they are on top of market fluctuations during their trading time.

Moreover, it is highly recommended to refrain from leaving open positions overnight. This is especially true in overseas markets with a significant time difference such as European or Asian markets. When a trader clocks out for the day and goes to bed, they cannot react to any type of fluctuation. Therefore, leaving open positions unattended only exposes traders to unnecessary risk.

**Day trading options**

Options are another type of derivative. Options hold a stock as the underlying asset.

Options have two positions called "put" and "call." A "put" option consists in selling a stock a specified price while a "call" option consists in buying a stock at a specified price.

Options are often considered to be risky and complex procedures. Options also require traders to make solid assumptions regarding the trend of a stock's price. If properly assessed, an option can help a trader make money based on the fluctuations of a given stock. In a way, it takes the guesswork out of buying and selling as the contract only kicks in at the specified price points.

In addition, options are good for day trading since it allows traders to take on contracts during the trading day itself. This type of trade can become lucrative during periods of high volatility. During periods of relative stability, options would offer limited possibilities for day traders.

Options contracts may have longer terms, but as stated earlier, leaving open positions for longer than a trading day, even for several days, opens the door for increased risk due to volatility. Nevertheless, one huge advantage of options is that the contract only kicks in when the specified price points are hit.

If an investor purchases a stock at $10 and places a put option at $12, the options kick in when the stock hits $12. This means the investor made $2 on the trade. However, if the price of the stock falls, then the put option will not kick in, and the investor is on the hook for the falling stock. Depending on the type of contract, the investor may not be able to sell to anyone else other than the other party in the options contract. As such, options can prove to be riskier trades.

**Day trading equities**

Lastly, equities, or stocks, are the most commonly traded financial asset.

Equities consist of buying and selling stock of publicly-traded companies. Basically, money is made when investors buy at a certain price and then sell at a higher price. During times of market volatility, equities may represent important opportunities to make money.

Highly-coveted stocks may offer "safer" opportunities but offer day traders limited opportunities to make money since potential increases in share prices may not be as significant as expected. A day trader may choose to throw their hat in the ring in the days prior to earnings calls and forecasts. Depending on these reports, top companies may experience spikes in share prices which day traders can take advantage of.

Other types of equities which day traders can choose to seek are called Penny Stocks. Penny stocks consist in equities which have a share price less than a dollar. They may also include companies with very low share prices. These equities represent buy low, sell high potential. Since day traders open and close positions on a daily basis, day traders can "nickel and dime" their way to steady profits.

Another type of equity trade consists of purchasing value stocks. These are stocks whose market value is below its book value. With these stocks, day traders may find hidden gems that are either undervalued or poised for a rebound after a rough stretch. If done right, value stocks can provide investors with the opportunity to make serious gains. Best of all, day traders can horn in on significant gains while closing their positions once they have made money.

Since equities are the most commonly traded assets, there is a wealth of information, data, and analytics available to traders. This wealth information can be utilized in making informed decisions that would enable investors to use their judgment and intuition in making savvy investment decisions.

## Chapter 2: Trading basics

In the previous chapter, we focused on the individual qualities that a trade must possess in order to become successful at day trading.

In this chapter, we're going to begin taking a deeper look at the way financial markets work. In particular, we're going, to begin with the basics of trading.

Financial markets function just like any other market. For thousands of years, markets have been places where buyers and sellers come together in order to exchange goods and services. In ancient times, markets were the scene of barter. Barter consisted of both the buyer and seller exchanging one good for another. For example, one individual would exchange corn and receive shoes in return. This was often a complicated process in which determining the proportion of corn and shoes that could to be exchanged depended on a host of psychological factors.

In the modern marketplace, buyers and sellers use money as a means of exchange. This means of exchange facilitates trade whereby, both buyers and sellers, are able to use money in order to buy or sell goods and services. And so, financial markets are no different.

In essence, trading, in any way shape or form, is nothing more than trading one security in exchange for money. Money is then used to purchase another security. That security can be resold in exchange for money again. This process is the essence of trading. The outcome of all participants in financial markets is to build as much wealth as possible. This well is expressed in terms of money.

Also, there are winners and losers in all financial dealings. Nevertheless, under ideal market conditions, all investors could potentially come out ahead.

Now, Let's take a look at the basics of a trade.

## Bid and Ask

When you look at stock prices, you will often see the reflection of what the market average is for that particular stock.

For instance, when you hear that a company's stock has reached $100, $200, or $300, for that individual stock. But just like any other trade, there must be a buyer and a seller. In addition, the stock market sets prices through supply and demand.

The law of supply and demand consists in both buyer and seller coming together at the market and determining the price of an individual stock based on a mutual agreement. This mutual agreement is as simple as comparing the price the buyer is willing to pay and the price the seller is willing to accept.

This is where the terms bid and ask come into play.

The buyer places the bid. The bid is the price that the buyer is willing to pay. In that regard, the bid is a reflection of the buyer's maximum price. This expected price is based on the average price of an individual stock. The buyer determines a specific price that they are willing to pay since this would enable trades to become profitable. The ask price is an expression of the seller's minimum accepted price.

I'm the other hand; the ask price is the price that the seller is willing to accept. Likewise, ask price is based on an investor's expectations and current market trends. If a stock has proven to be successful, the seller may have a higher ask price. Also, if the stock has been underperforming the seller may be willing to set a lower ask price.

The difference between the bid and ask price is known as the spread. Just like any negotiation, there will always be a difference in the buyer's expectations and the seller's expectations as well. If you have ever negotiated the price of any object, you will understand how this works.

Of course, there are times when buyers and sellers cannot agree then the deal does not go through. Most of the time, buyers and sellers are able to meet halfway and close the deal.

It's important to note that the spread is a key indicator of liquidity of the stock or security question. In other words, the smaller the Sprite, the better the liquidity. That means that a highly liquid asset will be easier to trade albeit at a lower profit.

The bid and ask price are not just limited to stocks and equities. They can be applied to Futures contracts options or even currency trades such as FOREX.

## Types of Orders

In stock trading, there different types of orders that are placed when completing trades.

So, Let's take a look at the different types of orders.

The first is a market order. This type of water consists of buying or selling the stock for security. This order ensures that the action will happen but does not guarantee a specified price. When the market order is placed it will usually happen at close to the bid price for a buy order, and close to the ask price for a sell order. However, there is no guarantee that when the market order goes through it will be at a price specified by the investor.

The second type of order is a limit order. A limit order depends on a specific price to buy or sell the security. The limit orders function is to set a maximum price for a purchase or a minimum price for sale. So, A buy order would only happen if the price of the security is lower than the bid price. In addition, a sell order would happen if the price exceeds the minimum ask price.

The next type of order is known as a stop-loss order. The stop-loss order consists of an immediate sell order when a stock reaches a specified price. So, if a stock falls the stop-loss order considerably would be triggered, and the stock will immediately be sold through a regular market order.

The last type of border is noun is a buy stop order. This order is triggered when the price of a security exceeds current market price. Therefore, the purchase does not happen. A similar order can be issued to stop the sale in order to protect the profit on a stock.

# Chapter 3: Setting up a brokerage account

This chapter will focus on brokerage accounts. Specifically, we will discuss the need for a brokerage account, the benefits of having one, and a way to set up one so that you can begin trading.

It's important to note that not all brokerage accounts are created equal. In fact, there is a considerable amount of research that goes into determining which account would be the best for you. That being said, doing your homework on the different types of accounts and the incentives available to you will pay off in the long run.

Traditionally, all stock trades went through a human broker. A human broker is a licensed professional who has the legal authority to conduct trades in the stock exchange on behalf of investors.

Nowadays, human stockbrokers are not exactly needed. The internet has enabled the average investor to set up an online brokerage account and begin trading on their own. Of course, the outcomes of those trades are solely the responsibility of the individual investor.

As such, a brokerage account consists of having excess to a trading platform offered by a financial institution. These financial institutions must be licensed to operate as authorized by the Securities and Exchange Commission (SEC).

Once an individual investor has set up a brokerage account, they will need to fund that account with actual money. The amount of money needed to fund an account will vary from account to account. Generally speaking, brokerage accounts can be opened with as little as $500. Furthermore, brokerage accounts enable investors to keep their proceeds deposited in that account, or they may choose to withdraw any amount of money in excess of the minimum needed to keep the account open.

The use of a brokerage account and an online trading platform are the two biggest requisites for a day trader. Without them, it would be virtually impossible for a day trader to conduct business in financial markets. They would have to become a licensed stock broker and work with a financial institution that operates in a stock exchange.

One of the biggest positives about using brokerage accounts and online trading platforms is that day traders can work from home, or virtually anywhere in the world, and conduct business in the stock market of their choice.

When shopping for a brokerage account, traders should consider all of the tools that come with that account. The brokerage account may include the use of the trading platform and access to all the analytics and data that are offered by the institution granting access to that platform.

Also, traders should look at the costs associated with the account and the use of the platform. Generally, accounts will charge a flat fee per trade. In addition, some accounts will charge a maintenance fee for the use of the trading platform and any other services that are associated with that account. In this regard, it's highly recommended that traders be aware of all the hidden costs that might come with that specific brokerage account.

If a trader is unaware of the hidden costs that come with the account they have chosen, these will add up and could potentially zap any profits that have been made through successful trades. Consequently, it pays to do your homework.

Now let's look at an overview of how a brokerage account works.

## Overview

As we have mentioned earlier, a brokerage account is a way in which investors can actively trade in financial markets. License brokerage firms offer brokerage accounts. This could be through banks or other fully licensed financial institutions. Any number of securities can be traded through brokerage accounts such as stocks, mutual funds, and bonds.

Once an account has been set up by the investor, now turned trader, they are free to engage in active trading. Even though the account is operated through a licensed brokerage firm, the trades themselves are the responsibilities of the individual investor. Consequently, the investor is the owner of the assets allocated in that account

That being said, a brokerage account is nothing more than a means to invest. The account enables investors to buy and sell assets traded in financial markets. Since not all accounts are created equal, a considerable amount of effort must go into researching the best options available to you as an investor.

So, Let's take a look at some of the elements that must be considered when shopping for an investment account.

## Fees

The first element that needs to be considered when shopping for an account is associated with fees. These are nothing more than the amount of money that the brokerage firm will charge for the use of your brokerage account.

In general, most firms have a similar fee structure. The actual dollar amounts that are charged for the for the account will vary from firm to firm. As such, let's take a look at the three types of fees that are usually charged by brokerage institutions.

- **Brokerage fee**. This type of fee consists of an annual or monthly fee that is charged in order to maintain the account. This fee is basically charged in order to keep the trading platform or system running. Depending on the account, this may include specialized information, research, data, and analytics which investors can use in order to conduct trades. Some brokerage institutions will choose to have a flat fee while others may choose to charge the fee based on a percentage of the account's equity or trades conducted.
- **Management fee**. The difference between a brokerage fee and a management fee is the person who is managing the account. If the individual investor is managing the account, then there will generally be no management be charged. If the investor chooses to have the assistance of a money manager, then they may be on the hook for paying a management fee. This management fee could be a flat rate charged on a monthly or annual basis, or it may

consist of a percentage of the account's balance. Some firms offer a combination where the individual investor can manage most of the account while seeking the assistance of a professional manager for other types of transactions. In that case, the investor would only pay a management fee associated with the assets the manager is responsible for.
- **Transaction fee**. Transaction fees are charged every time a trade happens. For example, when an investor buys or sells a security in a trade, it will have a transaction fee attached to it. Like in previous cases, a transaction fee may be a flat rate charged per trade, or it might be a percentage of the value of the trade. It goes without saying, that a trader who makes a lot of trades may see transaction fees pile up. That is why it is fundamentally important to keep transaction fees in mind.

## Account Minimums

Another fundamental characteristic a brokerage account is known is an account minimum. Since brokerage accounts come in all shapes and sizes, account minimums will vary considerably from account to account, and from institution to institution. Some accounts may require thousands of dollars to join while other accounts may only require a few hundred dollars.

In some cases, some accounts may require a little as $500 but may have a higher maintenance fee to make up for the lower minimum. These accounts may also have a higher transaction fee. On the other hand, some accounts that have a higher buy-in may offer a lower maintenance fee and lower transaction fees.

It's worth noting that account minimums are very important to keep in mind. If your account should fall below the account minimum, an additional fee for keeping a balance lower than the stipulated amount may be charged.

A good rule of thumb is to keep your account minimum in mind in order to avoid getting hit with unneeded fees.

### Requirements

Also, keep in mind that some brokerage institutions may ask investors to meet a certain set of criteria before becoming eligible to open an account with them. Basic requirements could include a social security number, being legal age, providing proof of employment, among other basic requirements.

Other institutions may require investors to meet certain criteria associated with net worth, amount of investable assets, or cash reserves needed to cover potential losses.

## Cash or margin

Another key characteristic of brokerage accounts if the ability to operate on cash and/or margin. Some brokerage accounts will require investors to deposit a certain amount of funds and will limit them to trade based on the amount of funds they have available. Once funds run out, they will not be able to trade unless they add more funds to the account. When an account is set to margin, the investor will have the opportunity to trade a certain amount without having any funds in the account. The margin assigned to the account will depend on the type of account. Of course, the investor will be asked to cover that margin at a specific point. If the investor is unable to do so, then they may be hit with additional fees or even suspension of the account until they can cover the margin they have used up.

## How to open an account

Once you have done your homework on the brokerage accounts out there, you can then proceed to open an account. While it is a fairly straightforward process, you do need to meet some requirements and submit some paperwork in order to get off the ground.

So, let's take a closer look at what you need to produce in order to get your account running.

- **Submit paperwork.** As with most financial matters, you will need to submit paperwork as required by the brokerage firm. Basically, you will be asked to submit paperwork in order to prove your identity, your social security number, proof of employment, a driver's license, financial information such as net worth, or any information the brokerage institution deems necessary.
- **Complete application.** Then, you will be asked to fill out an application. This application is a written statement of all your information. This is the official document that you submit in order to request access to your brokerage account. The institution then processes the application. Processing times vary from institution to institution.
- **Add funds.** Once the application has been approved, and the account is ready to go, you will be asked to fund the account. This can be done electronically via a bank transfer, or through depositing a check.
- **Conduct research.** The next step would be to look at the investment options available to you. This may include the wide array of investment

vehicles associated with the firm, or the market in general. This is where you can begin to test out the data and analytics tools that may be available to you. I recommend setting up a watch list so you can track trends before jumping into the investment.
- **Trade.** This is a big moment. This is where you complete your first trade using your new account. Logically, your first trade will be a purchase. Depending on your investment philosophy, you may choose to close all your positions at the end of the trading day or leave your positions open and track the behavior of your investments.

The process described above seems straightforward and does not require an extensive amount of legwork. What it does require is for you to be aware of all aspects related to your new account. For example, you need to be aware of fees, account minimums and any other charges associated with that account.

Furthermore, day traders should consider a brokerage account that has a lower transaction fee since opening and closing positions in a single day may represent several trades throughout the course of the trading day. So, bear in mind that transaction fees add up and can cut into your profits.

## Advantages of brokerage accounts

Perhaps the single most important advantage is that brokerage accounts offer a tremendous amount of freedom to traders. Since the trader is the only responsible for the transactions conducted in the account, the decision of where to allocate the account's funds depends on the experience and judgment of the investor.

With that in mind, it's important to consider that brokerage accounts will always have the edge over any other investment account that's managed by brokers and agents. The reason for this is that professionally managed accounts will kill you with fees. In addition, brokers will use their judgment in the allocation of investable assets. Thus, your opinion may not count for much.

Brokerage accounts also enable investors to trade when they are able to. If you, as a trader, need to take some time off, you have the freedom to do it. The account will be there when you choose to resume trading.

One other key advantage is that some brokerage accounts have a lower buy-in as compared to a traditional investment account. Often, traditional investment accounts have buy-ins in the tens of thousands of dollars.

With a brokerage account, the buy-in is a fraction of what a professionally-managed account would require. On top of that, the job that a regular stockbroker can do isn't that much better than what a day trader can do. So, brokerage accounts will allow you to reduce the management fees charged by money managers.

## What to watch out for

Lastly, there are several things to keep an eye on when you are shopping for a brokerage account.

- **Full-service account or discount account**. Full-service accounts generally offer greater support and tools. You get access to all the data and analytics that the brokerage firm has to offer. This may include insider research and other specialized advice. Some accounts even offer special training sessions. Discount brokers charge less, but also offer less. In the long run, a discount broker may end up leaving the investor out in the cold.
- **Shop around for fees**. A comparison of fees charged by different firms will enable you to see the pros and cons of each account. So, it pays to take the time to do some solid research. That way, you can have a clear idea of how your finances will play out.

- **Available investments**. Not all firms trade the same investment vehicles. So, it's important for you to be sure that your chosen firm trades in the investments you are looking to deal with.
- **Resources**. Make sure that you are aware of the resources that each account offers. As stated earlier, some offer more than others. So, it pays to do research on each one.
- **Experience**. Getting reviews from other users will allow you to get a picture in your mind about what kind of experience you can expect with your chosen institution's accounts and platforms.
- **Perks**. Some brokerage institutions will offer a series of perks in order to get you to sign up. Find out what they can offer to entice you to sign up.

One final thought: you shouldn't feel married to a given account. While you may be required to stay on board for a fixed period of time, don't be afraid to switch if you need to. There are plenty of options out there to choose from.

# Chapter 4: How to choose the right stocks

Choosing the right stock might seem like trying to call the weather.

Financial markets are often unpredictable, and at times, highly volatile. This is why choosing the right stocks boils down to having access to the right information and then knowing what to do with that information.

In addition, there is a myriad of indicators, variables, trends, among other dates, which you can use to make your analyses leading up to an investment decision.

The biggest piece of advice that I can give is to stick with what you know at first. For instance, if you are familiar with tech companies, then starting out with tech stocks would make the learning curve a lot more manageable for you. If you are the kind of person that is up to date on the latest gadgets and are familiar with the business implications of new technologies, then trading tech stocks exclusively at the outset may provide you with a good boost.

In addition to being familiar with the ins and outs of a specific industry, there are also a set of indicators which you must become acquainted with in order to make savvy investment decisions. By understanding this information, you will be able to get a better picture of where a specific stock may be trending.

Best of all, the indicators that we will discuss in this chapter are not dependent on specialized subscription services or any insider information. These are usually available in the mainstream business media. So, you won't have a hard time getting the information you need.

## Company revenue

In order for you to make a wise investment decision, you will need to become familiar with the financials of publicly traded companies.

But, fear not. If you are not familiar with financials or aren't too financially inclined, this is a great place to start.

The first financial indicator we will discuss is company revenue.

In short, a company's revenue is all the income that a company gets. The most typical source of income for a company is sales. However, there are other sources of income such as interest paid on deposits, royalties from patents, tax refunds, among other non-sale sources of income.

The determination of revenue is the result of a company's accounting process. This process is carried out by a company's accounting staff and is reported quarterly. It is important to note that publicly traded companies are required to present earnings reports every quarter. This is why some of the hottest tradings happen around the time of quarterly reporting. Here is a general guideline of when earnings reports are expected:

- Mid-January: Q4 (previous year)
- April: Q1 (January to March)
- July: Q2 (April to June)
- October: Q3 (July to August)

Needless to say, earnings season is always a hectic trading time since the results published a company will have a direct impact on their stock. Many investors will even purchase options in order to lock in trades based on the fluctuations of stocks during this time.

In addition, earnings reports are publicly available. Some companies choose to publish these reports on their websites. However, it is not a legal requirement for companies to do so. So, the safest bet is to check out the SEC's website. It contains links to the financial statements of all publicly traded companies.

It is highly recommended that you take the time to go over the financial statement of any company you are interested in buying. It is time-consuming, but the consolidated balance sheet, audit notes, and executive summary will enable you to get a clear picture of a company's financial position without digging too deep into their actual financials.

## Earnings per share

The next financial indicator to keep in mind is known as earnings per share.

This indicator is a proportion between the earnings, or revenue, of a company divided by the number of outstanding shares.

For instance, if ABC Company has reported earnings of $10,000 and it has 1,000 outstanding shares, the then earnings per share can be calculated as 10,000 / 1,000 = 100. In this example, the earnings per share are $100 per share.

It is important to note that this indicator should not be confused with dividends. Earnings per share indicate how much of a company's revenue corresponds to each outstanding share. A dividend is the amount of money shareholders receive from the company's profits at the end of a fiscal year.

Consequently, a company may post solid earnings per share results, yet it may not pay out a dividend because it has actually taken a loss instead of making a profit. On the other hand, if a company is doing well and generating profits, investors will receive a check for the dividends they are entitled to at the end of the fiscal year.

## Return on Equity

Return on equity refers to the amount of money corresponding to profits divided by the company's equity, or capital, at the end of the fiscal year.

In order to determine a company's equity, the following equation must be used:

## Assets (-) liabilities = equity

In this formula, assets can be considered as anything the company owns. In addition, assets include rights a company has to collect on a debt. For example, if a company has sold "X" amount of goods on credit, the company has the right to collect on that credit. This is known as "accounts receivable," and it is an asset. Assets include vehicles, inventory of goods, office equipment, buildings, among other non-tangible assets such as patents and intellectual property.

Liabilities are essential anything a company has to pay. For example, outstanding loans and payments due to suppliers can be considered as liabilities. Liabilities are also classified as short-term and long-term. Short-term liabilities are those which mature in a year or less, while long-term liabilities mature in a period greater than a year.

The end result of this equation is equity or the company's book value.

Let's consider this example:

ABC Company has total assets of $1,000 and total liabilities of $750. So, 1,000 (-) 750 = 250.

In this example, ABC Company's equity, or book value is $250.

Now, if we assume 1,000 outstanding shares, then the stock's book value would be 250 / 1000 = 0.25. This means that each share of ABC Company has a book value of 25 cents.

Let's also assume that ABC Company posted a profit of $500 at the end of the fiscal year. So, we can proceed to calculate the return on equity in the following manner:

Profit or loss/equity

In this case we have: 500 / 250 = 2. In other words, the return on equity for this example is 200%.

This result indicates that ABC Company is in a strong financial position which ensures its sustainability in the long run.

Since you are now familiar with the calculation of this indicator, you can always run the numbers yourself to make sure that the information you are reviewing is accurate.

## Analyst recommendations

I have always encouraged family, friends, and associates to take analyst recommendations with a grain of salt.

There are hundreds of analysts out there working independently or for large investment firms. These analysts will crunch the numbers based on the financials provided by companies and economic data. Based on their results, they will issue recommendations on which stocks are performing well and which ones are not.

Depending on the individual analyst of the institution they work for, they will have more or less credibility. Therefore, it is important to take analyst recommendations and check up on this information. Often, new investors will take analyst's recommendations at face value and base their investment decisions on this so-called expert advice.

If you do not follow up on expert opinions, you may find yourself exposed to risk. Now, I am not implying that analysts are wrong or manipulate information. While there have been cases of this, a wise investor, or trader, will always follow up any recommendations with their own analyses. In this way, you can determine if what you are hearing is a bunch of baloney.

## Positive earnings

Positive earnings refer to the trend observed over a period of time with regard to a company's earnings.

Being able to identify this trend is crucial in making appropriate investment decisions. When you detect a positive earnings trend, it means you have found a solid company with a good track record. While it's natural for solid companies to have a down year here and there, the overall trend should be an indicator of how well that company has performed over a specific period of time.

It is highly recommended for you to go as far back as the information allows. But a good rule of thumb is to look at the last 10 years of date. This will enable you to see where the company is heading. If you detect a solid company that has had a couple of bad years, you might be looking at a company that's poised for a rebound. This may represent a good investment opportunity.

In contrast, companies with a downward earnings trend are better left alone. Unless you can get into this type of stock cheaply, buying companies like this with the hope of a turnaround may end you leaving you with a few lumps. Early on, it's best to stay away from stocks such as these. As you gain more experience, you will be able to determine if it's a worthwhile investment, or not.

## Earnings forecast

This can make or break a company.

Earnings forecast are what market analysts expect a company to report. This forecast, or prediction, is based on historical data, current market conditions, and any other factors which may play in according to analysts.

These forecasts are issued by independent analysts, business intelligence companies or investment firms. The forecast issued by analysts will draw a line in the sand. Subsequently, if a company reports earnings above forecasts, then you can be sure the stock will gain momentum.

Conversely, if a company reports earnings below analysts' expectations, then the stock will most likely take a hit. The severity of the hit will depend on how bad the company missed the target.

Of course, this isn't an exact science, and there is no way to accurately predict what actual earnings will be. Nevertheless, forecasts are based on solid data and clear assumptions. So, take the time to familiarize yourself with earnings forecasts and keep an eye on your stock during earnings seasons. If analysts consider that a stock will beat expectations, then you might want to put in a position. Otherwise, steer clear of the losers.

## Earnings growth

This is another indicator that tracks a trend over time. Earnings growth is a reflection of a company's management and its tendency for growth and expansion.

This trend also enables investors to see whether a company has peaked, or if it still has room to go. A flattening earning growth trend most likely means that a company has reached a peak. So, unless they are able to produce a change that will spur growth, companies may flatten and then go splat. These types of stocks will provide little to no value.

On the other hand, if you see that a company has had a decent growth trend, but has had a bad year, then you might be able to get quality stock on the cheap. You can then flip when things turn around.

This information is generally available though you could visualize trends just by looking at a company's balance sheet over the last ten years. You only have to focus on its earnings account. There is no need to focus on additional information. Of course, a more thorough analysis will lead you to look deeper into other parts of a company's financials.

One word of caution: beware of companies that haven't shown much growth and then suddenly spike. When this happens, it is usually due to singular events which have caused the company to increase its earnings. Unless the spike is part of an overall growth trend, you may have an outlier on your hands. Thus, you might want to stay away from it. Although, you could capitalize on the buzz and flip the stock while it is still up; just be careful you are ready for the next earnings season.

## PEG Ratio

The PEG ratio stands for Price/earnings to growth ration.

This ratio is a measure of how well a stock has been performing as compared to its expected growth. In other words, it is a measure of how well a stock has met expectations.

This is an ideal measure for companies that have a clear growth trend. Nevertheless, it is a great way to measure any company's performance over time. It should be noted that the higher the PEG ration, the better growth potential a company exhibits.

Also, this ratio is a measure of the value of a company's stock base contrasted with its actual growth. This ratio is also considered to be more complex as compared to the traditional P/E ratio, which is, price to earnings ratio.

The traditional P/E ratio takes a company's stock price into consideration and divides it among a company's earnings. This is why the PEG ratio is more complex as it considers growth. Moreover, the PEG ratio is a much more accurate indicator of a company's growth trend as opposed to the P/E ratio.

## Industry price earnings

This indicator builds on the individual P/E ratio calculated for a company and contrasts it to the industry-wide ratio. So, the P/E ratio can be calculated for an individual company and an entire industry.

The industry P/E ratio represents an aggregate measure of an industry's performance a whole. It is the sum of all of the companies in a single industry.

The industry P/E ratio can serve as a baseline for individual companies. So, if a given company has a P/E ratio above the industry average, you can be sure that this is a solid company. In contrast, if a company shows a P/E ratio below the industry average, then you may need to dig deeper to see why this company is underperforming.

It worth noting that industry averages are not entirely representative of individual companies. For example, an industry may be dominated by a single player and then made up of multiple, smaller players. This is why it's always a good idea to look at the P/E ratio of the biggest player in an industry. This will enable you to see just how wide the gap might be between the top player and other players in the same industry.

Therefore, taking a look at the biggest company will allow you to see just how representative the industry-wide P/E ratio actually is. Perhaps you might find better value within the smaller players than in the bigger ones.

## Days to cover

The final indicator to consider in this chapter is called days to cover. This measure consists in determining the number of days short sellers have to cover their positions.

A short sale consists of an investor purchasing an asset and then flipping it to another buyer, hopefully, at a higher price. Nevertheless, the investor has a set amount of time when they need to pay up for the purchase of the stock.

If the short sale was successful, the investor should have enough cash to cover the position. However, if the stock should drop in value, the investor may have to sell immediately in order to cut their losses. This is why short sales are some of the riskiest investment strategies out there.

The days to cover ratio can be measured by taking the current short interest and dividing into the average daily volume. In addition, a short seller may use stop-loss orders to prevent getting hammered in case the stock they are shorting falls below their expected level.

Short sales are not recommended for longer-term investors. In fact, short sales are quite good for short-term investors particularly when a stock has seen some volatility. When shorting stocks, investors must be keen not to hold on for too long; otherwise they will be forced to cover, and they may not have the funds to do so.

Well, we have certainly covered a lot in this chapter. I know that it was full of financial discussion that you may not be familiar with. But the good news is that there are training courses that build on the concepts presented in this book.

Also, investors should become familiar with companies' financial statements. In particular, you should become familiar with balance sheets and the information they contain. Also, P/L statements, or profit and loss statements, will enable you to see where a company is heading.

Financial statements are not only readily available, but they are the best source of information on a company's financial health.

By law, publicly traded companies must present audited financial statement. That means that external auditors must independently verify the information presented by a company. Since the Enron scandal of 2001, external audit firms have been held to extremely tight standards. Thus, it is safe to assume that the information presented in a company's financial statements is as accurate as humanly possible.

So, don't fear financials. This section has provided you with the most important aspects you need to understand in order to evaluate stocks accurately. With this in mind, you can feel reassured that you have made your investment decisions based on solid financial information.

Moreover, you will be able to take analysts' forecasts and recommendations and see for yourself if what the pundits are saying in actually true. You have all the tools you need at your disposal; it's just a matter of understanding what to do with them.

To get started in learning more about companies' financials, I suggest you visit company websites. If they have no financial information available, you can peruse the SEC's website to see what information is available on any given company.

# Chapter 5: The best time to trade

Day traders, by definition, open and close their positions within the same trading day. Thus, there are not open positions overnight.

We have discussed how this investment strategy can help day traders sleep better at night as they can go bed knowing that there won't be any surprised in the morning awaiting them.

Now, during the trading day itself, there are specific points in which you might see more, or less, activity. Also, there are certain points where you will notice greater gains or greater losses.

## Overview

Generally speaking, markets open around 9 am. While this isn't cast in stone, it's a general rule. Understanding this is important since trades are happening all over the world while North America is getting a good night's sleep.

A good indicator of what's to come on a given trade day is the trend on the international futures market. For example, the trend seen in the futures market in Asia will help give an indicator of what to expect in North America the next day.

For those who trade in FOREX overnight currency operations in overseas markets will enable day traders to see what's up ahead for that trade day. This is why leaving positions open overnight can pose a serious risk.

Allow me to elaborate further.

Let's assume that you are trading futures. A futures contract is a type of derivative that seeks to lock in the price of a commodity in advance of its actual delivery.

The best example of a futures contract is oil. Oil is bought and sold today but delivered three months later. So technically, investors are trading something that doesn't exist yet. The oil will come into existence when it is pumped and then shipped to the refineries.

Now, if you decide to buy an oil futures contract, you may close out your day with one price point. However, oil futures took a hit in the Asian markets while you were comfortably asleep.

Bear in mind that whatever happened overnight will not affect you until the trading day starts up again. After seeing what happened in the Asian markets, investors holding oil futures and oil ETFs may choose to get out immediately. So, they are not going to wait long. These investors will dump their futures and ETFs as soon as the opening bell hits.

So, unless you are up really early, you may miss the action and see your investment plummet.

As you can see from this example, leaving positions open overnight will leave you vulnerable to the effects of overseas markets. That is why closing your positions at the end of the day will allow you to get a good night's sleep.

## Market opening

In the previous example, we discussed how investors dump what they don't want right at the beginning of the trading day. Therefore, the biggest losses happen at the beginning of the day. And, the biggest bargains can be found at the beginning of the day.

Let's assume that you have been tracking a stock that's been on a downward trend. You can choose to set a price point to buy. You might even purchase an option that will trigger a buy order when the price falls to your specified point. When this happens, you could find yourself getting the deal you wanted on a stock you have been tracking.

Then, as the trading day progresses, you will find that markets tend to rebound and recover from opening losses.

The opposite is also true. When there are positive news from overseas markets, the opening of the market in North America may see a significant jump. You may choose to get in immediately and sell quickly before the momentum wears off. This might prove a bit risky since you need to time the purchase and sale quickly. This may mean that you will hold on to a position for only a couple hours, if not minutes.

So, I would encourage you to check the trends of overseas markets first thing in the morning. This will enable you to develop your strategy for that trading day.

## Market closing

You might be surprised to hear that the biggest gains are made at the end of the trading day. This is true since most investors are looking to close most, if not, all of their positions by the end of the day. So, it is the last couple of hours in a trading day that tends to be the fastest and most furious.

Let's assume that you got a good deal at the beginning of the day. Since you managed to get some quality stocks at a good price, you are sitting back and tracking the momentum in that stock. Suddenly, you might see that stock beginning to climb right around 2 o'clock pm. That might be the signal that it's getting to be time to sell.

Once the stock has passed your designated sell point, it's time to pull the trigger and call it a day.

Thus, market closing generally tends to be a great time to sell especially if you are not keen on having open positions overnight.

If you are a swing trader and keep positions open overnight, then the end of the trading day may provide you with some bargains since the increased selling action may actually push the price of some assets down. This is particularly true of stocks that have been underperforming, or simply haven't bounced back. Investors who want to cut their losses or just close out for the day may choose to sell at whatever price point they can manage.

## Avoiding pitfalls

The biggest pitfall to avoid has to be following the crowd. Mob mentality has led many investors to get into stocks that aren't going anywhere. Unfortunately, day traders and average investors may go ga-ga over a stock pick recommended by a television analyst. This may trigger a frenzy for that stock. Needless to say, this isn't something you want to be a part of.

In addition, having access to credible sources of information is the best way for you to make wise investment decisions based on solid data and analytics.

Day traders should also stick to their game plan. It might be tempting to hang on to stocks for a couple of days. But unless you are certain, as much as you can possibly be, that the trend observed in that stock will last as long as you anticipate, it's best to just cash out at the end of the day. It is the best thing you can do to ensure your mental health.

# Chapter 6: Reducing risk in day trading

Managing risk is a key element in any successful investment strategy.

Experienced investors understand the importance of managing risk in such a way that they are able to foresee the potential drawbacks that come with engaging in any type of trading in financial markets.

So, risk is a vulnerability which leaves an investor exposed to a negative outcome. Consequently, vulnerabilities represent the potential for a negative outcome thereby creating a negative condition that will adversely affect your desired results.

Based on this logic, a risk is a potential negative outcome. That means you must do everything you can to manage that potential situation and become aware of how you can reduce the likelihood of that negative condition from taking place.

Experienced investors understand where potential pitfalls may hide and what they can do to avoid them. Often, they are aware of these pitfalls because they have fallen into them. Other times, wise investors learn from others' mistakes and are able to identify the same potential risks in their own trading activity.

In this chapter, we will take a look at some of the vulnerabilities which you need to look out for during trading. By addressing them at the outset, you can ensure that you will be one step ahead of these potentially negative outcomes.

In addition, you will begin to build your business acumen to a point where you can automatically detect when you are exposing yourself to risk.

Now, we have address risk throughout this book so far. This is why I have advocated the validity of becoming a day trader.

Why?

Well, I have underscored numerous times how vulnerable you become when you leave positions open overnight. By closing your positions before the end of the trading day, you have managed risk in such a way that you take the uncertainty away from your investment.

By opening and closing your positions every day, you are certain of what your current situation is at all times. In a way, it's providing peace of mind for yourself. So, if you had a bad day, you can put it behind you and move on. If you had a good idea, you can build on that success and keep rolling the next day.

Whatever your circumstance, leaving open positions unattended is opening the door for trouble. This highlights the biggest risk that could ever affect you: not being able to react in time to changing market conditions.

If you are not physically able to deal with situations as they happen, then you are setting yourself up for potential losses.

Let's consider an example:

You are trading FOREX.

FOREX is highly volatile, meaning that fluctuations can happen unexpectedly and can hammer you without prejudice.

So, let's say that you are trading US dollars and Euros. This currency pair seems harmless enough as neither currency has been experiencing significant fluctuations. As such, the spread margins are rather narrow. That means that your gains, or losses, won't be significant, but given the right timing, you can make a few bucks on each trade.

Now, let's assume that you open and close your position every day. Whatever your outcome, win or lose, you are clear on what your position is.

However, you decide that these two currencies are stable enough for you to leave your position open and allow market fluctuations to play overnight. You can always resume trading when you wake up in the morning. Unless you are planning on sleeping for four hours, this leaves you vulnerable to the fluctuations of European markets which trade overnight.

Let's assume further that the European Central Bank has announced an interest rate and investors begin dumping the Euro in favor of other currencies such as the Swiss Franc, US dollar, or even gold. If you are holding Euros, the value of your investment can fall rapidly zapping any potential gains. If you were at your trading station when the news broke, you could react quickly and make the trade accordingly. But since you are getting a good night's sleep, your reactions may come too late.

This example shows how things can quickly change and leave little time to react.

As a result, taking a proactive approach in dealing with risk will enable you to better protect yourself against potential risk while cutting your losses should things get that far.

## Determining the right amount of investable capital

Determining the amount of money you should put toward trading is about as tricky as trying to decide how much money you should gamble away in Las Vegas.

The easiest part is understanding that you shouldn't bet the farm. Often, investors seek not to just hit a home run, but a grand slam.

As I've mentioned earlier, it is possible to hit a grand slam and clean up. It is possible though it rarely happens. The reason for this is that you would need to invest a considerable amount of capital and have the profit on a trade be such that it multiplies your original investment.

That being said, putting the entirety of your investable assets into trading all at once exposes you to unnecessary risk. Now, I am not saying that you will lose all your money and end up broke. But it should be noted that such things do happen when investors get reckless.

I have always advocated a gradual approach in which you can build up your equity at a moderate pace. In doing this, you will ensure that whatever market conditions prevail, you will not lose the farm should the worst happen.

So, I would encourage you to look at the account minimums that brokerage accounts require you to put down. Based on that, you can decide which amount you are willing to gamble away. The way I see it, think of the money you are going to invest as the amount of money you would be willing to blow in Las Vegas. That is, assume that you are going to spend a weekend at a casino, and you are perfectly fine in blowing that money on the experience of playing at a casino.

When you keep that attitude, you are not emotionally invested in the outcome of your trades. You will not feel pressure to succeed since you are comfortable with the idea of losing the money.

Does that mean that you should play to lose?

Of course not!

It just means that if you invest a considerable sum of money, you will feel the pressure to win every trade. Consequently, being under that kind of pressure may cloud your judgment and lead you to make trades that you might not be entirely comfortable simply because there is a lot at stake.

That is why I always encourage folks to avoid betting too much, too soon. If you are completely new to this game, small, incremental steps will ensure that you will have a solid strategy. Eventually, you will be able to build up enough equity so that you can engage in larger trades. As you gain experience and recognize the opportunities available to you, you will be able to hit home runs consistently. After all, the best home run hitters don't start out hitting the ball out of the ballpark. They have to strike out a few times before getting the big hits.

## Setting up a stop-loss point

We discussed stop-loss points earlier when referring to the types of orders available in investing.

A stop-loss point basically consists in drawing a line in the sand in which you decided that when the stock hits that point, you will automatically sell.

A conservative approach might be to set up your stop-loss point slightly above your purchase price. Therefore, you will ensure that you won't lose money on the deal even if it means making a slight profit. Also, you could go even lower and set your stop-loss point at your purchase price so that you break even.

This approach is set to ensure that you don't lose money on deals. However, you could be a bit more aggressive and set your stop-loss point below your purchase price. The reason for this is that it will give you a bit more time for the stock to rebound even if it's trending downward. The logic behind this approach is that if a stock falls low enough it will trigger multiple sell points and the stock will rebound.

This is a risky approach since there is no sure-fire way of knowing how far a stock would fall. In fact, if you set your stop-loss point too low, it could fall below the stop-loss points of other investors. This means that you will never recoup since a large amount of sell orders will drive the price of the stock further down. By the time your sell order kicks in, you'll have a 50/50 chance, at best, to catch the rebound.

So, when deciding to set your stop-loss point always ask yourself how low you are willing to go? The answer to that question will determine your stop-loss point.

## Working with a broker

Financial firms employ brokers to be full-time managers for their client's assets. As such, brokers are experienced individuals who have a clear understanding of how trading works, the risks and the opportunities that may become available to investors.

Passive investors are always willing to pay a bit extra for qualified brokers who have a solid track record in asset management. This is something important to consider especially if you are new to the investing game.

By working with a broker, you are not admitting that you can't do it yourself. What you are recognizing is that the broker's experience will help you reduce the risk of losing money while you learn the ropes of the markets. Consequently, seeking their advice can as much a learning experience as a way of protecting yourself.

Naturally, this advice doesn't come for free. However, you may want to look at what your brokerage account includes. Full-service accounts may include advisory sessions with a licensed broker who can assist you in making the right deals. This is usually part of the maintenance fee you pay for your account.

Other full-service brokerage accounts offer training seminars, webinars, or even one on one coaching calls. So, it pays to look into a full-service brokerage account.

On the flip side, discount accounts will most assuredly not offer any type of support. In that case, you may want to seek out professional advice on an hourly rate. This will ensure you the coaching you need and provide you with direct access to an experienced, licensed professional.

One word of advice regarding online training courses: online courses by so-called experts are not always 100% accurate. While they may not be intentionally misleading, they may be off in their assessment of financial dealings. Therefore, it is always a good idea to consult with different sources before heeding any financial advice. One good rule of thumb to follow is to make sure that anyone who is giving you financial advice is a licensed broker. If they give you the wrong advice intentionally, the will lose their license. So, beware of anyone who is not duly licensed.

## Taking breaks when needed

Taking a break is not a risk in itself. The risk is pushing yourself too hard.

When investors take day trading on as a full-time occupation, discipline is needed in order to keep a balanced schedule. Some traders may choose to log on right at the start of the trading day, take a break for lunch and then jump into the afternoon session.

However, being a day trader doesn't stop there. There is a considerable amount of time and effort that needs to be put into research and study. This is where becoming a trader can get overwhelming. That is why keeping a healthy schedule can ensure that you will always have a fresh mind.

Nevertheless, there is a point where you need to take a break from it all. Finding the right time to do so can become challenging. Since your livelihood will depend on the results you are able to produce from trading, you will need to make sure that you have enough money set aside to cover your expenses while you are not trading.

When you become truly successful, you will be able to save up some money for such occasions. Some traders choose to take a couple of days off here and there just to unwind and clear their minds. Since markets are open from Monday to Friday, you can close your positions on Friday evening and close the shop for the weekend.

There is something to be said about taking long vacations as a day trader. sBeside the fact that you may not be producing any income when you are on vacation, being away for too long may disrupt your mojo. Now, this doesn't mean that you shouldn't take a vacation at all, it just means that even if you take a break, you would do well not to take your eye off the ball.

The good thing about day trading is that you can essentially do it from anywhere in the world so long as you have an internet connection. Thus, you could potentially go on an extended holiday and plan your trading day around other activities you wish to do or places you are planning to see.

Remember that one of the main reasons why investors become day traders is so that they can have the freedom and the flexibility to work anywhere at any time.

### Keeping emotions in check

Hollywood films often portray stock traders as flashy and flamboyant individuals who wear their hearts on their sleeves.

The truth is that being a stock trader requires individuals to have nerves of steel. Often, there are situations in which traders need to keep a cool head while exercising sound judgment. Those individuals who let their emotions get the better of them may end up making ill-advised decisions regarding their investments.

Keeping emotions in check is part of the self-discipline that traders must exercise. Self-restraint is important particularly when emotions run high during bull runs or crashes. Many investors get caught up in the frenzy when other investors are clamoring to buy or sell.

In particular, market crashes tend to bring out the worst in people.

Take the market crash of 1929. Many investors lost everything but the shirt on their backs. This devastating situation motivated the suicide of ruined individuals. Fast forward to 2008, and the great financial crisis was an exercise in greed by bankers and investors while ordinary citizens got caught up in the cheap money available to them.

These are examples of how emotions can cloud an individual's better judgment. Consequently, one of the most fundamental traits of any investor is to keep their head during times of euphoria and hardship. By setting stop-loss point, or placing options are automatic devices which investors can use to protect their positions from unexpected swings.

One other important aspect, investors who are able to keep their cool will learn to see value and opportunity under circumstances when others are panicking. Furthermore, panicked investors make rash decisions. These are the conditions which savvy investors can exploit to their advantage.

## Avoiding fads

Fads and trends are dangerous. Investors who follow the crowd often expose themselves to unnecessary risk. When investors choose to get into an investment vehicle when it's "hot," it means that the opportunity to make money on that investment in long gone.

Since the price of investments is driven by supply and demand, inflated asset prices occur when a large number of buyers decide to get in. At this point, the original investors have already cleaned up. What's left is a string of investors chasing the same nickel.

The best time to get into investments is in the early stages. For instance, when companies are in their startup phase provides the best opportunity for investors and venture capitalists to get the most value for their buck. When companies eventually make it to their initial public offering (IPO), these initial investors can clean up when the next round of investors gobble up the stock. Even those investors who pounce on the IPO can clean up when the stock's price gains momentum. By this point, the more recent investors will make a pittance on it.

The moral of this story is that great value can be found when investors go against the tide. When an investor decides to follow the crowd, they are only feeding the frenzy. When an investor chooses an alternative path, the opportunities for finding hidden gems increase significantly. Of course, this requires greater research, but the potential upside is definitely worth it.

In addition, investors who keep their emotions in check will be able to extricate themselves from market fads and make wise investment decisions based on their personal investment strategy while focusing on achieving their individual goals.

The points described above allow investors to manage risk. It is clear that risk is an inherent part of investing. So, there is no way to avoid it completely. The best investors can do is manage risk in such a way that there is a clear strategy defined in case the worst should ever happen.

At the end of the day, experience is the best teacher. Those investors who learn from their mistakes, and those of others, can gain valuable skills in managing risk and protecting their assets. Moreover, keeping a cool head is the best way that investors can reduce their exposure to risk. When investors do not exercise restraint in their actions, their better judgment becomes clouded. This impaired judgement can lead to making a riskier investment. As we have discussed earlier, riskier investments expose investors to even more risk. Unless an investor is experienced and fully comprehends the mechanics of the investment vehicle, it's best to play it safe. Inexperienced investors may be able to dive into the deep end as they gain experience and build momentum.

# Chapter 7: Day trading strategies

Becoming a successful trader is part art and part science.

The artistic side trading consists in developing and intuition for potential opportunities and being able to sniff out hidden gems where others may not be able to find them. This artistic ability is developed through years of experience and lessons learned. Often, investors rely on their instincts in order to figure out where golden opportunities may lie.

However, investment trading isn't just about intuition or sniffing out opportunities. In many ways, being a successful trader depends on utilizing available data and analytics in order to make a trade based on solid and relevant information.

So, in order to take advantage of available data and analytics, investors need to become familiar with the statistical tools that are available to them. This information may come from business intelligence information offered by brokerage firms through their accounts. Other sources of information include the mainstream media and dedicated business channels and analysts.

At first sight, the myriad of information available to investors may seem overwhelming. The constant flow of information may cause the novice investor to feel overloaded with data and numbers. Consequently, it is important for investors to have a clear picture of what all of this information means in order to sort through it and use it to their advantage.

We will present a series of statistical tools that are available to investors so that they can make wise investment decisions based on solid empirical data. But, there's no need to worry. We are not going to get into the specifics of how to calculate each one of these statistical tools. We will, however, discuss what they are used for and how we can trip with them so that the next time you see them, you will be able to get the most out of the information presented.

The most important thing to keep in mind is that practice makes perfect. So, the more you brush up on business intelligence information related to the stocks you're interested in dealing, the more you will become familiar with their patterns, trends and overall direction.

## Candlestick charting

One of the elements in the job description of an investment trader is learning to read charts. There are several types of charts which investors must become familiar with. For example, statistical data in graphs illustrate the trends and patterns of financial markets. These are presented in just about every report pertaining to stock markets.

In this section, we're going to look at one very specific type of chart which is named the Candlestick Chart.

Candlestick Charts consist of a statistical model that takes into account the link between price and supply and demand. This link is presented in a chart that is comprised of a number of boxes, which resemble candlesticks and represent the trend of the price of an individual stock.

The Candlestick Chart contains four components: the low price, the high price, open price, and the close price. These four elements come together to produce what is known as a Candlestick Chart. This chart represents the price range of a stock with regard to its open and close price for that day.

Regular Candlestick Charts have two types of depictions. One is a black body, and the other is an empty body. A Candlestick Chart with a black body represents a price range whereby the close price was lower than the open price. In theory, this means that the stock lost value throughout the trading day. If the Candlestick body is empty, then that indicates that the close price was higher than the open price. In other words, this means that the stock gains in value throughout the trading day.

The candlesticks themselves can be color-coded in order to determine when the price has gone up, or when the price has gone down. Generally speaking, investors prefer to use red, instead of black, to indicate that the price has done down. Also, some investors prefer to use green in order to indicate that the price has gone up.

## Bullish candlesticks

When referring to market trends, investors use the term "bull market" to indicate that the market is strong, and it is gaining in value. As such, bullish candlesticks refers to candlesticks which indicate a positive trend in a market.

In essence, the bullish trend can be observed when buyers outnumber sellers. In that regard, the law of supply and demand will determine that when buyers outnumber sellers, prices will go up based on the scarcity of the good. Buyers will be willing to pay more and more for a scarce good. Unless the good is so abundant that the number of sellers is irrelevant, prices will always go up whenever demand outpaces supply.

It's important to note that rising equity prices are always an indication of a bull market. Therefore, investors can utilize the data provided by the upward trend of candlesticks in order to call the trend bullish.

One other note: an individual stock may be deemed bullish even if the entire market itself is down. When markets are down, that does not necessarily mean that all stocks are down. In fact, some stocks benefit from a bad market. For instance, stocks that have consistently maintained low prices would become attractive to investors due to their lower value. This may prove to pay off when the markets begin to recover.

## Bearish candlesticks

The term "bear market" is used when markets are down. As such, a bear market indicates that the overall market trend is downward. This trend is reflected in the price of equities as they are down from their previous highs.

The rule of thumb used to call a bear market consists of a market reduction of at least 20% from its previous high. This implies that a bear market will emerge when the overall trend of a market has been down for at least 20%.

The same principle applies to individual stocks. When a stock price faces a downward trend, its candlesticks will reflect this trend as well. Therefore, bearish candlesticks indicate that the stock is losing value. This trend can occur regardless of the prevailing market conditions. So, even if the stock market is booming, an individual stock may show signs of losing value.

In general terms, an individual stock may become bearish when supply outpaces demand. In this case, there are more sellers than buyers. Consequently, sellers must accept a reduced price in order to sell their equities. The more sellers there are in the market, the more the price will be pushed down.

It's worth noting that when a stock enters the bear market territory, an investor must decide whether it's better to hold on to the stock and wait for a rebound or sell short and cut losses. The most important consideration in this regard is that bearish trends must be taken seriously, and positions must be closed in order to prevent considerable losses.

## The ABCD pattern

The ABCD pattern is a statistical model that uses data in order to determine the potential of long positions. In this case, long positions refer to the purchase of the stock whereby the investor will take an equity stake in the stock.

In general, the ABCD pattern utilizes intraday data to measure the trend of the stock. In addition, this model factors in a set risk for the stock in question. It also measures what is known as a breakout level.

In short, the risk level is the set point where the stock will fall below an investor's expectation while the breakout level is the point where the investors' expectations are surpassed.

The ABCD patter consist of four points:

- A: The stock breaks past its initial high and sets what is known as an "intraday high." This is the point that determines the "breakout" level.
- B: The stock then registers a reduction and fall from the breakout level. This is where the stock set what is known as an "intraday low." This low point is what sets the "risk level."
- C: The stock has a quick, but short-lived, rebound and falls back close to risk level.
- D: The stock then takes off again and breaks through the breakout level.

As you can see, the stock shows a pattern whereby there are peaks and troughs in the stock's price curve. This trend will produce a jagged line which is indicative of this pattern. Ultimately, the investor would be able to make a profit when the stock's price reaches the "D" point.

The trend described above corresponds to a bullish pattern. This means that the stock has shown signs of trending upward. However, the ABCD pattern may also show signs of a bearish trend.

In this trend, the ABCD pattern is the opposite of the bullish pattern.

In the bearish pattern, each one of the points indicates turning points in the downward trend in the stock. As such, the bullish pattern indicates the best time to sell whereas the bearish pattern indicates the best point to buy. Consequently, the bearish pattern can be used by watching a stock that you are looking to purchase. When the stock hits point "D," that would be the best time to buy it.

So, in the bullish pattern, A is high, B is low, C is low, and D is high. When the stock hits "D", it's time to sell.

In the bearish pattern, A is low, B is high, C is high, and D is low. When the stock hits "D", it's time to buy.

The ABCD pattern is a staple of short-term traders who are looking at intraday movements of stocks.

## Reverse trading

Analysts closely watch reversals in order to determine the point in which a stock's trend will reverse into the opposite direction. For instance, if a stock is trending upward, the reversal will reflect the point in which the stock will begin a downturn. Likewise, when a stock is trending downward, a reversal would indicate the point in which the stock will begin an upward trend.

Traders and analysts keep a close eye on the candlestick movements of a stock in order to detect a potential reversal. Since the candlesticks refer to the range between the lowest and highest prices of a stock through the trading day, a potential reversal may be evident.

When the potential for a reversal is indicated, it may indicate the right time to go long, or short, on a stock. If an investor is holding on to a stock, the may choose to sell at the top, that is, at the highest of the stock's price right before the downward trend is set to begin.

Also, an investor may closely track the downward movement of the stock and buy right at the bottom, that is, the lowest point of the trend right before the stock is set to pick back up. This is a classic example of the buy low, sell high strategy.

When a trader is able to determine potential reversals, they may decide to put in an option and buy or sell, at a specific price point. This would ensure that the trader does not miss each of the points where the reversal might take place.

## Moving average trend trading

A moving average is a statistical tool that looks to flatten out fluctuations in a given data set in order to establish the trend of a stock price.

This tool constantly updates a stock's average price by recalculating the stock's average price at consistent points through the trading. In doing so, the statistical model that is generated enables the investor to determine a stock's trend throughout the day, or even longer term such as weeks, months or perhaps years.

The moving average strategy reduces the fluctuations in a given data set. So, if you are tracking the behavior of a stock for the last month, you will be able to see a trendline emerge. This trendline cuts out the fluctuations and leaves a smoother, flatter line which would indicate an upward, downward or sideways trend.

Common longer-term calculations can be expressed in a 50-day, 100-day and 200-day moving average. When longer-term trends emerge, the lower point in the average price of stock is called the "floor", that is, the support for the stock's price, while the highest point in the average is called the "resistance level", that is, the highest point in which the stock is looking to surpass.

Floors and resistance levels often trigger automatic buy and sell orders. These are key psychological milestones which investors use to determine the overall performance of a stock.

## Resistance trading

As indicated in the previous section, the highs and lows of the moving average for a stock set what is referred to as the floor and resistance level.

Both floors and resistance levels are psychological barriers which trigger buy and sell orders. In this regard, investors may choose to purchase options on the pre-determined floor or resistance levels. This is why stocks tend to trade in a specified range.

So, when the stock is close to the resistance level, sell orders and triggered which push the price back down. Conversely, when the stock is close to hitting the floor, buy orders are triggered, and the stock price starts to climb back up again.

To break through both the floor and resistance levels, external factors need to influence investors' mindset so that they can decide to pursue trades beyond the floor and resistance level observed in the price of an equity.

## Opening range breakout

Range trading is one of the first strategies that novice investors engage in. This is due to the fact that ranges are easy to spot. In this sense, investors can quickly spot when prices fall outside the range as evidenced by recent trends.

Investors can use candlesticks or moving averages in order to determine a stock's trading range. Therefore, traders will react to any situation where the price of a stock falls either below the floor or breaks through the resistance level.

As previously indicated, prices below or above the high-low points will trigger market orders. However, one of the most useful strategies is called the opening range breakout. This strategy consists in acquiring a stock when the opening price falls below the stock's floor.

This type of strategy is a staple of day traders since traders open their positions every day. Often, stocks open at lower-than-usual levels. This would enable a trader to make some considerable gains when the stock rebounds.

In order to set yourself up to an opening range breakout, you must track the trend of a stock right up until the close of the market. That trend will enable you to figure out if the stock will open at a lower point. This is a stock which you could keep a close eye on.

### Red to green trading

This strategy is another staple of day traders. As opposed to opening range breakouts, red to green trading is focused on the close of the day.

In essence, this strategy consists in keeping track of a stock which has been negative for the day and then purchasing right at the end of the trading day. This is possible since a stock that starts out in the red and then moves into green throughout the day will get a boost from an influx of traders looking to make a few bucks right at the end of the day.

This strategy is all about timing. So, it's best to set your buy-sell points so you can be sure that you will not miss on the changes in the stock's price. In addition, this strategy will enable you to close out strong at the end of the day and perhaps make some extra bucks that you didn't expect on making.

## Data analysis in trading

Data analysis is the core of successful traders. Day traders, in particular, live and die by the numbers. Thus, if a stock's movements are consistent with certain parameters established in your trading strategy, you can decide to buy or sell. That comes with a keen understanding of the data related to that stock.

The good news in all of this is that most data analysis is already done for you. So, you won't need to look at complex data sets and crunch the numbers yourself. In this regard, there are a wealth of sources which you can count on to provide you with reliable data and analysis. Often, your brokerage account will come to access to data and analytics. Consequently, you will have the option to use that information in order to make savvy trade decisions.

## Technical analysis in day trading

Much like data analysis, technical analysis plays a key role in trading.

Technical analysis includes any type of analysis which is related to understanding a stock's trend. This implies understanding statistical data on the stock's price. Also, this implies understanding the nature of the company itself along with the broader economic context of the economy.

Technical analysis is all about utilizing statistical models in order to establish a stock's trending behavior in addition to understanding the range in which it is trading. There are several instruments which can be used in order to conduct a technical analysis. These tools will be covered in depth in the next chapter.

Chapter 7 covered a series of strategies which are rooted in technical analysis. Hence, it is vitally important that all traders become familiar with the various statistical models at their disposal. By understanding how these models work, investors can gain a clear understanding of how financial markets work based on the analysis of price ranges.

However, traders also need to gain a broader understanding of the world around them. This broader understanding encompasses other aspects such as politics, macroeconomics, behavioral economics, among other non-statistical factors that may influence investors' attitude at any given point in time.

For instance, political instability and turmoil wreak havoc on investor's minds. As such, investors may be more inclined to play it safe since uncertain conditions are not generally conducive to positive outcomes.

On the other hand, if a country has released positive information on its economy, job growth, and debt levels, then investors will feel more confident in investing and will choose to allocate more resources toward trading. These psychological effects all stem from a technical analysis of a host of variables that come into play within financial markets.

It is highly recommended that investors become as familiar as they can with the technical aspects of the markets they are trading in and becoming keenly aware of each stock traded. This implies additional research. Nevertheless, positive research is never a waste of time.

## The bottom line

This expression refers to a company's profitability. As indicated before, a company's financials are essential in determining whether the stock will be sought after or disregarded by investors.

However, the bottom line also applies to investors. The main motivation for investors is making as much money as possible. So, investors need to become aware of the importance that the bottom line has on their decisions. This means that investors are in it to win it. Consequently, decisions should be made on what is best for your financials. This implies taking emotions out of the equation.

Please remember, when investors keep a cool head, they are able to use their better judgment to make solid investment decisions. When their emotions drive investors, they are only setting themselves up for failure.

# Chapter 8: Advanced trading strategies

So far, we have discussed everything from market basics to analytics to some of the most battle-tested trading strategies. As such, the information discussed has been intended to get your trading strategy off the ground.

At this point, we have come to discuss advanced strategies that will enable you to get the most out of your trading activity.

In this regard, the strategies discussed in the chapter are "advanced" trading strategies. This means that these strategies are used by seasoned investors who have developed a solid understanding of financial markets, trading, and analysis.

One word of caution: the strategies discussed in this chapter will allow you to get the most out of your efforts but are not recommended for novice investors. It is recommended that you attempt to implement these strategies after you have gotten your feet wet and have a solid understanding of how your investment strategy translates into your investment decisions.

## Gap up, inside Bar, breakout strategy

This strategy depends on the analysis of candlesticks. In this case, the "bars" (candlesticks) reflect the trend of a stock's price.

Since each bar is tracking a stock's price range, the initial bar, also referred to as the "mother bar" serves as the reference for future trades. The mother bar set the high and low prices that will determine the action to be taken.

Based on the mother bar, the next price point is called the "inside bar." The inside bar consists of a new bar set within the range of the mother bar. As such, the inside bar is literally "inside" the range of the mother bar. What this strategy enables traders is to set buy and sell points that reflect the range established by the mother bar.

It's important to consider that inside bars are always relative to the mother bar. And since the mother bar is the reflection of a given range within any definite period of time, the mother bar can be calculated at any point during the trading day.

The use of bars within a trading strategy should be encompassed within the market's overall trend. So, inside bars can be used to trade in accordance with the market trend. This is called a "breakout play."

A breakout play is when the inside bars trade within the direction of the market's trend. When the market is trending upward, inside bars will reflect an upward trend in the individual market price range of a stock. This strategy makes sense when the trend is clear, and there is very little volatility in the market.

When markets show considerable signs of fluctuation or volatility, investors may choose to play it more conservatively and focus only on the mother bar – inside bar trade.

In addition, bear in mind that this strategy is based on a gap up. In other words, this is when a stock opens the next day at a higher price than the close price of the previous day. The difference between the final close price and the new, higher opening price is called the gap.

When gaps are larger than expected, investors may choose to hold on to their positions a lot longer than they normally would. In the case of a day trader, this might mean holding on to a stock for the entire trading day.

## Gap up, attempt to fill, breakout

Under this scenario, a stock has moved up from the previous day's close. The gap up at the opening of the new trading day is what investors are looking for in order to drive their breakout strategy.

However, when a stock goes from a gap up back to the previous day's closing price, the reduction in price is known as the "gap fill." When the gap is filled, the stock's price is generally reacting to resistance levels.

For instance, a company that reported higher than expected earnings the day before may experience a gap up on the next trading day. But since the stock's price meets a resistance level set by investors, it may "fade" back to its previous high. In this case, the gap has been filled.

When investors attempt to take advantage of the gaps, they are "playing the gap."

There are several ways to play gaps. The most popular play is by shorting stocks. When an investor decides to short a stock, they are looking to play the gap when it is filled.

It is highly recommended that investors take care in watching price behavior when playing the gap before taking a position. Inexperienced investors may choose to take a position right at the opening of the trading day. While there might be a possibility that the stock's price may continue to rise, there is also the possibility that the price of the stock may revert and start filling the gap.

This is where savvy investors can play the gap and put in a position when they feel the stock has come back down to its low point.

The main takeaway of playing the gap is that trades must always be in the direction of the price. So, if the price is trending upward, then that's the way the trade should go. Furthermore, it is highly recommended that investors closely check the stock's movement in order to determine when the gap might start to fill. This type of tracking may require an investor to check in on the price every 10 minutes.

Once the stock has filled the gap, a breakout play may occur when investors' buy positions are triggered, and the stock begins to gain momentum. So, it may very well pay off to place a call option at the beginning of the trading day and set a put option close to the end of the day.

## The gap up, afternoon breakout

In this approach, the gap up at the beginning of the trading day is the reflection of the previous day's trend for that stock. When the stock's trend reverts and begins to fill the gap, stop-loss orders may become triggered.

By the time the stock is done filling the gap, most investors who played the gap up may have already gotten rid of their position leaving the stock to trade within its traditional range.

In this regard, investors may choose to keep a close eye on the candles for that stock. If they detect the candles trending back upward, the stock might be poised for an afternoon breakout. Consequently, investors may end up waiting close to the end of the trading day in order to take long positions. This will trigger the afternoon breakout.

It's worth noting that afternoon breakouts generally tend to happen when the cause for the gap up is related to solid fundamentals and not black swans.

For instance, a gap up might be caused by better than expected earnings. This has come to be a welcome news to a firm that had been struggling in recent quarters. So, investors flock to get a piece of the action. The gap up is subsequently caused by irrational behavior on the part of some investors.

When institutional investors begin to liquidate their positions in that stock, the gap will continue to fill. Investors may dismiss the earnings call as a one-off, and the stock looks unlikely to rebound and will continue to trade within its usual range.

Given the same circumstances, a stock might be poised for an afternoon breakout if investors deem the earnings call to be a sign of better things to come. In this case, the gap fill is a logical consequence of the sell orders triggered by the new high point in the stock. If the stock continues trending upward throughout the day, a new floor might be set, and the resistance level has taken higher.

In this example, the stock may very well exhibit and ABCD pattern and break through resistance levels at the end of the trading day. Thus, investors must be wise in setting this buy-sell points effectively in order to avoid being caught unawares.

## Fibonacci retracement pattern

This tool is used as a statistical analysis of a stock's price. In short, it is used in an attempt at setting the floor and resistance level of a stock.

The Fibonacci retracement pattern is based on the famous mathematical concept known as the Fibonacci sequence. This sequence is made up of the following in numbers: 0, 1, 1, 2, 3, 5, 8, 13, 21, 34, 55, 89, 144... Basically, the sequence consists in starting with the number 0 and then adding the next number with the previous number in order to generate the next digit. So, 0 is first, and then it is followed by 1. These two numbers are added, 0 + 1, to produce the next digit which is 1. The next digit is 1. So , 1 + 1 = 2, and then 1 + 2 = 3, 3 + 2 = 5 and so on.

As such, the Fibonacci retracement pattern uses the Fibonacci sequence in order to produce the following ratios: 23.6%, 38.2%, 50%, 61.8%, and 100%. The most common ratio is 61.8% as it is the result of dividing one number with its previous number. For example, 21 / 34 = 0.6176 or 61.8%. This ratio holds up with the numbers contained throughout the sequence.

Next, the high and low points of a stock price are taken, and levels are set based on the Fibonacci ratios. So, the 100% level would be the highest point while 0% would be the absolute lowest level in the price trend of that stock.

Then, lines are drawn to represent the 23.6% level, 38.2% level, 50% level, and 61.8% level. These points can be used to attempt to establish the floor and resistance level of a stock. Of course, it is not foolproof, but the use of this sequence has proven to be useful in identifying general trends.

In addition, for the Fibonacci retracement pattern to be successful, major peaks and troughs need to be used in order for the analysis to bear the desired outcome. Needless to say, this analysis has yielded rather accurate results over the course of its use in stock trading analytics. Investors would do well to become familiar with this sequence so that they can use their better judgment to establish their price points accurately.

## Gap down, fill down, inside bar, breakout

Throughout this section, we have discussed the concept of gap up. Now, we will look into the concept of gap down.

Gap down works much the same way as gap up does. The difference lies in that a gap down consists in a situation where a stock's opening price is lower than the previous day's close. As such, the price is down. When the gap begins to fill, the stock's price begins to rise back to its usual trading range. This type of behavior may be the result of an ABCD pattern that extends of two trading days.

The reasons for a gap down are numerous. Let's consider an example:

A company received negative earnings forecast. Analysts are forecasting this company's earnings report to fall under expected levels. As a result, investors began dumping the stock as at the end of the trading day. When the markets opened the next day, the stock got hammered as the previous day's closing price triggered stop-loss positions.

However, investors ultimately consider that these lower than expected earnings are nothing more than a bump in the road. So, they feel confident that even if the company does report lower than expected earnings, it will bounce back in the next quarter.

As such, investors begin tracking the inside bar of this stock and set up their buy options. It is quite probable that this stock has fallen into an ABCD pattern. So, the gap down could well have been point B. Now, the stock is poised for a rebound.

When the rebound comes, the stock is set to break out as the gap begins to fill. Once the stock has closed the gap and it reaches breakout level, a rush of buyers chooses to get back into the stock as they have heard analysts discussing that the lower than expected earnings is nothing more than a minor setback. At this point, the stock had a breakout and is trending higher than before.

The previous example underscores how psychology plays a fundamental role in determining how price points are set and how inexperienced investors will chase the trend. Thus, it is fundamental for investors to keep a cool head even when most folks are rushing back into a stock after it has rebounded.

At this point, we have covered a great deal of information regarding trading strategies. If you are feeling a bit overwhelmed, I don't blame you. I felt the same way when I first started out in trading. There is so much to take in and so much information to digest. This is why I advise you to take things slow.

That is why the strategies outlined in chapter 7 are ideal for investors who are new to the game. The strategies outlined in this chapter are perfect for more experienced investors. When you are able to combine both, you will become a savvy investor who will know how to react at all times. By keeping cool and rooting your investment decisions on technical analysis, you will be able to set yourself up for success and avoid falling into some of the most common pitfalls that new investors fall into. Ultimately, it's up to you to do your homework and make the most of the information available to you.

# Chapter 9: Tips for completing a successful trade

Well, we are almost at the finish line for this book. Since you've made it this far, you have already digested a considerable amount of information. You are now ready to begin your trading career. Even if you begin at the shallow end of the market, you will most assuredly have a leg up on scores of traders who don't know any better. In that regard, investors need to continue growing and evolving along with market conditions. This is a constant endeavor that will pay off down the road.

In this chapter, we will go over some final tips and recommendations for you to keep in mind so that you can boost your chances at of making successful trades more often than not. While it is true that you won't win every single trade, you can reduce the likelihood of losing by improving and building on your skills and knowledge.

So, let's jump into the following tips and recommendations for completing a successful trade.

## Building up a watch list

This is my first stop.

Building a watch list will help you keep track of stocks which are of particular interest to you. This list should contain stocks which you have been following for a set period of time but are not priced at a point you are comfortable with.

So, building a watch list with these types of stocks will help you visualize the trends in price. By visualizing these trends, you can see in which direction the stock is going. Whether the stock is trending upward or downward, you will be able to understand where it is going and at what price point you would be interested in taking a position.

Also, you can build watch lists according to an industry. For example, you might be interested in following certain tech stocks which appeal to you. You can look at the trends of individual stocks and then compare their patterns. This type of analysis will enable you to realize how well one stock is doing over another.

One other reason for building a watch list may be related to a certain event you are expecting to happen. For instance, you might be anticipating earnings season. Given that earnings season is a significant event, you can set your watch list and track the movement of your preferred stocks right up until their earnings announcements.

The biggest advantage of building a watch list is that this list enables you to narrow your view. This poses a considerable advantage as compared to having a broad view of all stocks. By narrowing your view, you will be able to take advantage of specific opportunities. If you have too broad of a view, then you may miss out on a potentially lucrative trade.

### Deciding on the right stocks for you

Deciding on the "right" stock isn't easy.

Often, investors may become focused on a specific stock or industry. When this happens, investors gain special insight into a given industry. This special insight allows investors to act both on intuition and data.

Also, experience is a key element in determining what the best stock would be for you. Through experience, you will develop a knack for a specific type of stock based on industry, turn of business, or even based on the management team running the company.

Deciding on which stocks to buy also depends on understanding the underlying information related to that company. This requires some additional research into an individual company. As I have stated earlier, research is paramount in developing a successful investment strategy. When you understand the company itself, and not just the analytics based on data, you can gain special insight into the direction this company will be taking.

I encourage investors to get to know the people running a company they wish to buy into. Often, companies are successful because they have the right management team at the helm of the company. Other times, once successful companies take a turn for the worse when new management takes over.

Furthermore, understanding a company's financial position will also enable you to gain special insight as to the direction a company is headed. This is especially true when companies run into debt issues. If a company has healthy financials, then you can be sure that their stock price will reflect that fact. On the other hand, a company with shaky financials met exhibits and equally shaky stock price. Investors are always wary of companies whose financials do not reflect sound management and clear direction.

That is why I stress the importance of research whenever the topic of choosing the right stock comes up. Don't be afraid to add several names to your watchlist. Your watchlist will be the perfect place to start picking the right stocks for you.

## Putting an entry and exit strategy into place

One of the cardinal rules in investing is knowing when to get out.

Inexperienced investors tend to hold onto stocks a lot longer than they should. Or, they tend to sell sooner than they should. That is why seasoned investors understand the importance of having both an entry and exit strategy. When referring to entry and exit strategies, we're not necessarily talking about leaving investments altogether.

What this strategy refers to is having a clear vision about when you will jump in and when you will push back and call it a day. Perhaps the hardest consideration with regard to having an entry and exit strategy is knowing the right time to buy in. Inexperienced investors generally make the mistake of buying into an asset at the top of its price. When you get into an asset at the top, or close to the top, you are setting yourself up for a massive letdown. When the price of an asset peaks, it has nowhere to go but down.

Earlier in this book, we discussed how important it was to avoid following the crowds. When you see in investors flock toward a specific stock, asset, commodity, or any other financial instruments, you are most likely too late. When investors all jump in at once, they drive up the price of any given asset. This creates a psychological phenomenon whereby prices are artificially inflated due to irrational behavior. Veteran investors will know that when other investors flock toward an investment they own, it's time to sell and get out.

In addition, exit strategies pertain to knowing when to cut your losses. Of course, we don't wish to have losses in any trade. But there is the very real possibility it's you will end up losing from time to time and as such, having an exit strategy can be something as simple as setting a stop-loss point. Or, you can set up a put option at the specific price point. When the equities you hold trigger this option, you will be in a good position to avoid sustaining losses.

One other point: investors keep a cool head at all times and know when the time comes to get out. Rational investors are able to keep their emotions in check and avoid making reckless investment decisions due to their ambition and greed getting out of hand.

## Purchasing desired stocks

Consistency is the staple of successful investors. Being consistent enables you to chart a course and follow that path in such a way where you will not deviate from it. Being consistent allows you to develop your own investment style. Moreover, it enables you to specialize in a particular sector or industry. As a matter of fact, specializing in one particular type of financial instrument will help you gain an edge over other investors.

By flip-flopping from one investment to another, or from one industry to another, you are only exposing yourself to unnecessary risk. The risk lies in making ill-advised investment decisions due to ignorance or perhaps a lack of judgment.

So, being consistent will enable you to find the right time to purchase the stocks that you really want to buy into. You will gain insights and understandings that come with experience and in-depth research. Consequently, you will not only get the stocks that you want, but you will also get them at the price you want. One crucial characteristic that you must exhibit in this case is patience. When you are looking to buy into stocks that you truly desire, having a clear entry strategy will enable you to get the stocks that you want at the right price. By succumbing rational behavior, you may end up overpaying for a stock that may leave you with disappointment and potential losses.

Therefore, when you set out to acquire a stock, or equity, that you truly desire, you can build a clear entry and exit strategy around that particular stock. You can begin by setting a price point at which you will buy in. That can become a great start to a successful trade.

## Paying attention to the market until the trade is completed

When you set out to make a trade, it's important to keep your eye on the ball at all times. Often, investors may relax a little too much when taking a position in a specific stock. If you happen to take your eyes off the ball, you might miss unexpected events that will cause you to become exposed to risk.

This is why day traders have a leg up another types of investors. Day traders are known for opening and closing their positions on the same day. This strategy enables them to cut out any potential risk that may happen while they are away.

The same principle applies to investors who engage in trades and disregard they're open positions during the trading day. I have underscored the fact that markets are often unpredictable and volatile. As such, anything can happen at any time of the day. By disregarding open positions, or simply relaxing too much, you might miss out on significant developments throughout the trading day. That may also lead to missed opportunities.

Of course, I don't mean that a trader should not even get up to go to the bathroom. What I do mean is that it is important for investors to keep their eyes and ears open at all times while they are engaging in a trading activity. In fact, I would even go as far as advising traders to close their positions before they go out for lunch. Again, markets are unpredictable, and anything can happen.

Also, are you, fine traders, to set up are buy and sell points well in advance so that automatic price points will allow traders to focus more on the action that's happening in front of them and not lose focus unfollowing individual price points.

Once your trade has been completed, and the money is in the bank, you can relax and enjoy life.

## Selling stocks when reaching original exit points

When you set up your sell points at the beginning of a trade, you have done so based on the fact that you have decided on a point where you're comfortable with selling. When you reach this point, it's best to go ahead and sell. There is always the temptation to hold onto a stock just a little bit longer in hopes the price will continue to go up. That is how many investors have crippled their profits.

Your goal should be to achieve the points that you have identified at the beginning of the trade. I have always said that it's better to be a day early than the day late. There is always that thought of "what if." For example, "what if I had waited just a little bit longer. Perhaps I could have made some more money on the deal". However, this is a dangerous position to put yourself in. When your stocks have reached the selling point that you have determined it's time to get out.

This is why I keep saying that it's important for investors to keep a cool head. When greed takes over, judgment becomes clouded, and investors tend to hold on to stocks longer than they should. In fact, you should sell at any point you are making money on a stock deal.

If it turns out that you could have made more money on the deal, I would advise you to go back and determine what was it that led you to make the decision to sell too soon. This retrospection will enable you to understand where you could have gone wrong and how to address that in future trades.

## Reflecting on trades and extracting lessons learned

One of the best investment strategies that I have heard of is keeping a diary. Investors who keep a diary can keep track of their trades and also keep track of their thoughts as they made those trades. This diary, or journal, then becomes a chronicle of the thought process that you have gone through in order to arrive at the investment decisions that you have made.

If you are wrong and have made mistakes, this journal will enable you to go back and see where you went wrong. This isn't an exercise in dissecting failures. Rather, it is an exercise in improving upon your investment strategies.

When you realize the mistakes you have made, the next step is to figure out the best way to address them, so they don't happen again.

Once again, a journal, or diary, is a great way of chronicling your thought process and how you evaluate stock deals. You can derive a trove of information from the lessons learned that you have distilled from both positive and the negative experiences.

The worst thing that you can do is to continue your trading strategy without properly reflecting on how you can improve it. Constant improvement and evolution are critical factors in becoming the best possible trader you can be.

Some of the best investors in history have learned from their mistakes. In fact, many professional investors appreciate failure insofar as it allows them to keep learning and gaining experience which will lead them down the road to greater success.

So, the next time something goes wrong, don't be afraid to go back to the drawing board and ask yourself what you could have done better.

## Researching information for future trades

Research is another one of the aspects that I have highlighted throughout this book.

Research is the lifeline that allows you to uncover potentially hidden gems that lie in financial markets. Furthermore, research will enable you to uncover potentially lucrative opportunities which other investors may have overlooked. As a matter of fact, it's quite easy to overlook potential opportunities when they're buried beneath a seemingly endless stream of data.

Of course, understanding and interpreting data is essentially seeing the forest for the trees. That is why your priority should be to have access to as many sources of information as you can. By having access to multiple sources, you can gain insights that a single source may not be able to provide.

Even if your first stop for information is the data and analytics service that your brokerage account provides, you can always seek out additional sources of information. I have always said that you can never have too much information.

Other times, having access to multiple sources of information allows you to cross reference data. By cross-referencing data, you can make sure that the information you are basing your decisions on has been duly processed and verified. If for some reason things don't go as expected, you can always go back and see where those data sources could have improved the information they provided to you.

Conducting constant research is a proactive attitude that will allow you to visualize where markets are going. Furthermore, on-going research will allow you to place an individual stock in the grander scheme of a market. When you can see how an individual stock plays in relation to an entire market, you can determine if you are getting the most bang for your buck or if you need to stay away from that particular stock.

## Automating trade processes

The human brain is an incredible machine. In fact, it is so remarkable that it is capable of processing volumes of information at the same time. However, there is such a thing as overwhelming your brain with data.

Every day, we are constantly bombarded with information from seemingly endless sources. The brain becomes very adept at filtering out information that it does not need. Otherwise, the brain would become impossibly cluttered with useless information.

That being said, online trading platforms enable day traders to automate many of the processes that they engage in on a daily basis. This automation reduces decision fatigue in traders. For example, an investor will choose to set their buy and sell points.

Once those points have been set, the investor can relax and focus on the events as they are unfolding. The automated buy and sell points trigger when the parameters are reached. Since this is an automated process, the investor has essentially made up their mind well in advance. If the investor should choose to go back on their decision, it might be too late since the system may not allow them to go back after a specific point.

I have also stated that it is important for investors to keep their eye on the ball. So, automating processes is not about taking your eye off the ball. Rather, automating processes is about reducing unnecessary distractions. Distractions can prove to be costly since they take attention away from things that truly matter. If you can make a decision, then put it behind you, and you will be able to focus on the next milestone ahead of you.

I would encourage you to take a deeper look at how the tools at your disposal can enable you to automate as many processes as possible. This will help free up your mind to focus on research and learning.

Attention is a scarce resource. As such we must learn to focus our attention into the directions that will lead us toward achieving our goals.

# Conclusion

Wow! I can't believe this book is already over. It seems like we started the introduction just a few moments ago.

But just because the book is coming to an end, it doesn't mean that your journey as a day trader is too. In fact, it's just getting started.

I am thrilled to see that you have made it this far because it means that you have read through everything this guide has to offer. As such, I feel that you are now ready to begin making your first trades.

Just a couple of final reminders:

- Keep cool. Don't let your emotion get the best of you.
- Stay focused. Don't take your eyes off the ball.
- Take a break. Don't be afraid to unplug when you need to.
- Do your homework. It pays to keep up your research.
- Play it safe. But also play to win.

These reminders are based on what I do myself. I believe in keeping cool even when things are getting pretty hard. Your focus will keep you on the right path. Furthermore, your motivation will gain momentum when you begin to see the fruits of your labor.

Keep in mind that you can do it!

There is nothing holding you back. The biggest obstacles that you will have to overcome are in your mind. But if you truly believe you can make it, you will. It's all a matter of having the will and determination to immerse yourself in the world of day trading. I assure you that when you see the first successful trades pop in your account, you will remember how hard it was for you to get started, but you will also understand how rewarding it can be.

Best of all, you will be well on your way to financial freedom and security. You will soon begin to build the life that you have always wanted. Best of all, it will be all thanks to your own hard work and efforts. You can feel proud of yourself because you set out to do something really hard that very few even try much less become successful.

You have already taken the first step. So now, it's time to roll up your sleeves and get to work!

I hope you have enjoyed this book. I also hope you have found it interesting and informative. So, please don't forget to leave feedback. Other interested readers will greatly appreciate your honest opinion. Also, it will serve to help me continue improving my writing and my delivery of content.

**Thanks again** and I will see you next time!

**Finally, if you found this book useful in any way, a review on Amazon is always appreciated!**

www.ingramcontent.com/pod-product-compliance
Lightning Source LLC
LaVergne TN
LVHW090807201224
799564LV00032BC/473